The Bible is weird and books about it are gener
coma. But I didn't fall asleep once while re:
Genesis—easily the Willy Wonka-est book in
best tour guides, this author is a little demented
Read this and see for yourself.

T0357275

—**HARRISON SCOTT KEY**, author, *How to Stay Married*;
winner, Thurber Prize for American Humor

Moses is a master storyteller, and Genesis is his masterpiece. Alex Duke does
this inspired book justice as he zooms in on overlooked clues and zooms out
to behold the progress in God's plan of redemption. Whether you think you
already know everything about Genesis or you don't know your Joseph from
your Jacob, this book will help you see the divine in the details.

—**COLLIN HANSEN**, vice president for content and editor in
chief, The Gospel Coalition; author, *Timothy Keller*

Alex Duke takes us on a tour of Genesis, explaining both the text and its con-
tribution to biblical theology. The writing is fresh, inviting, and captivating.
A perfect guide for those who desire to know the message of the book in the
Scriptures that is foundational for the entire biblical narrative.

—**THOMAS R. SCHREINER**, James Buchanan Harrison
Professor of New Testament Interpretation, and associate
dean, The Southern Baptist Theological Seminary

Many people equate Bible commentary with unpleasant medicine, but Alex
Duke wisely adds spoonfuls of sugar in *From Eden to Egypt*. His tour of
Genesis is perfect for both seekers and suspicious people who think the Bible
is for suckers. It's also enjoyable and instructive for longtime churchgoers and
Sunday school teachers.

—**MARVIN OLAKSY**, executive editor for News and Global, *Christianity Today*

One of the greatest challenges the church faces today is the crisis of Bible
illiteracy. The church has never had greater access to our sacred text, yet we
are paying less and less attention to it. There is no greater antidote to Bible
illiteracy than the Bible itself and resources like this. If you want your church
to grow in Bible literacy, then start with *From Eden to Egypt: A Guided Tour
of Genesis*.

—**JT ENGLISH**, lead pastor, Storyline Church; author, *Deep Discipleship*

The Bible is not boring, but sometimes we forget that. And by "sometimes" I mean almost daily. Sure, we say it's important (we've got copies on the shelf to prove it!), but the truth is we are intimidated—especially in the Old Testament—by its ancientness and complexity and size. Do I need a theology degree to understand this? In a word: no. Alex Duke is a normal person who has written, for normal people, a brilliant book about the Bible's first book. If you can track with Genesis, you will be positioned to treasure the rest of the story. Alex's writing fizzes with humor and verve—and remarkable insight. So, assuming you're a normal person, open these pages and revisit Genesis with him. I promise you missed stuff last time around.

–MATT SMETHURST, lead pastor, River City Baptist Church, Richmond, VA; author, *Tim Keller on the Christian Life* and *Before You Open Your Bible*; cohost, *The Everyday Pastor* podcast

Genesis is a beautiful, rich, and foundational book in Scripture. But it's also daunting and, for most people, difficult to understand. Alex Duke's *From Eden to Egypt* walks readers through Genesis in a way that's approachable, relatable, and—dare I say—even fun! Whether you're a church leader teaching through Genesis, a student looking to better understand God's Word, or simply someone curious about a pivotal but often misunderstood book of the Bible, *From Eden to Egypt* is a fantastic resource.

–BRETT MCCRACKEN, senior editor, The Gospel Coalition; author, *The Wisdom Pyramid*

The whole storyline of the Bible is embedded in Genesis, even if only in seed form. That's why *From Eden to Egypt* is such a tremendous resource and can help you better understand the entire Bible in all of its richness and beauty. Alex Duke writes with clarity, pastoral insight, and even humor in such a way that makes for a great read.

–MATTHEW J. HALL, provost, Biola University

Genesis is an amazing book, and Alex Duke truly succeeds in bringing it to life for the everyday man like me. This book is proof that theology books can be a rip-roaring good time. I pray that more theologians learn to write like Alex so that more Christians will take up and read.

–SEAN DEMARS, pastor; host, *Room for Nuance* podcast

I like books that are handles—books that give one a handle on big biblical books, books that show how it all fits and flows. And Alex Duke's *From Eden to Egypt* does that for Genesis. It's neither too light nor terribly labyrinthian but, like Baby Bear's porridge, just right. It's done in a style that's both whimsical and serious, with a blend of light touch and faithful focus on the text. It's a delightful piece of work.

–DALE RALPH DAVIS, former professor of Old Testament, Reformed Theological Seminary/Jackson; minister-in-residence, First Presbyterian Church, Columbia, SC

Alex makes a lofty claim early in the book that he wants to "write a book about Genesis for normal people." And then he follows through on it by explaining a complex story in a way that is easy to understand and even easier to relate to. It's somehow both funny and foundational.

–KYLE PORTER, founder, Normal Sport

Really encouraged! What a fluid, down-to-earth journey through the first book of the Bible. With a good dose of humor and plenty of aha moments, this book reminds me of the beauty and wonder of Genesis. Whether you're opening a Bible for the first time or you've read it a hundred times, this book will deepen your appreciation and understanding in a way that feels both approachable and inspiring.

–GRANGER SMITH, speaker; *New York Times* bestselling author, *Like a River*

There's no book like Genesis, and there's no guide like Alex Duke, whose voluble tour of Moses' masterpiece has all the sweep and specificity of a campfire story, the punchy expertise of sports play-by-play, the candor of personal testimony, and the spirited conviction of a great gospel sermon. God bless him. *From Eden to Egypt* is a marvel, a book as various, coherent, and surprising as its glorious source text.

–DREW BRATCHER, author; associate professor of English, Wheaton College

From Eden to Egypt combines the breadth of my favorite commentaries, the insight of my favorite biblical theologies, and the readability of my favorite magazines, all with a voice that's fresh and fun, but never frivolous. Alex has a keen eye for what questions we'll be asking, for what details will seem weird or confusing, and he comes right at them with explanations that give us exactly what we need. This is an unusually good book. I can't wait to share it with others.

–MATT MCCULLOUGH, pastor, Edgefield Church; author, *Remember Death*

FROM EDEN TO EGYPT

FROM EDEN TO EGYPT

A Guided Tour of Genesis

Alex Duke

 ZONDERVAN
REFLECTIVE

 9Marks

ZONDERVAN REFLECTIVE

From Eden to Egypt
Copyright © 2025 by Alex Duke

Published in Grand Rapids, Michigan, by Zondervan. Zondervan is a registered trademark of The Zondervan Corporation, L.L.C., a wholly owned subsidiary of HarperCollins Christian Publishing, Inc.

Requests for information should be addressed to customercare@harpercollins.com.

Zondervan titles may be purchased in bulk for educational, business, fundraising, or sales promotional use. For information, please email SpecialMarkets@Zondervan.com.

Library of Congress Cataloging-in-Publication Data

Names: Duke, Alex, author.
Title: From Eden to Egypt : a guided tour of Genesis / Alex Duke.
Description: Grand Rapids, Michigan : Zondervan Reflective, [2025] | Includes index.
Identifiers: LCCN 2024043572 (print) | LCCN 2024043573 (ebook) | ISBN 9780310159728 (paperback) | ISBN 9780310159735 (ebook) | ISBN 9780310159759 (audio)
Subjects: LCSH: Bible. Genesis—Commentaries, interpretations, etc. | Bible stories, English. | Christian life. | BISAC: RELIGION / Biblical Commentary / Old Testament / Pentateuch | RELIGION / Christian Ministry / Discipleship
Classification: LCC BS1235.52 .D85 2025 (print) | LCC BS1235.52 (ebook) | DDC 222/.1106—dc23/eng/20241025
LC record available at https://lccn.loc.gov/2024043572
LC ebook record available at https://lccn.loc.gov/2024043573

Scripture quotations unless otherwise noted are taken from The Holy Bible, New International Version®, NIV®. Copyright © 1973, 1978, 1984, 2011 by Biblica, Inc.® Used by permission of Zondervan. All rights reserved worldwide. www.Zondervan.com. The "NIV" and "New International Version" are trademarks registered in the United States Patent and Trademark Office by Biblica, Inc.®

Scripture quotations marked ESV are taken from the ESV® Bible (The Holy Bible, English Standard Version®). Copyright © 2001 by Crossway, a publishing ministry of Good News Publishers. Used by permission. All rights reserved.

Scripture quotations marked KJV are taken from the King James Version. Public domain.

Any internet addresses (websites, blogs, etc.) and telephone numbers in this book are offered as a resource. They are not intended in any way to be or imply an endorsement by Zondervan, nor does Zondervan vouch for the content of these sites and numbers for the life of this book.

All rights reserved. No part of this publication may be reproduced, stored in a retrieval system, or transmitted in any form or by any means—electronic, mechanical, photocopy, recording, or any other—except for brief quotations in printed reviews, without the prior permission of the publisher.

Cover art and design: Nick Perreault
Interior design: Sara Colley

Printed in the United States of America
25 26 27 28 29 LBC 5 4 3 2 1

To Mel,
whose love for and reliance on
God's Word changed my life.
I love you.

Great are the works of the LORD,
   studied by all who delight in them.
—PSALM 111:2 ESV

CONTENTS

PART FOUR: GENESIS 37-50

FOREWORD

If we compare the book of Genesis to an autobahn (no speed limits) that has both long straightaways, hairpin turns in mountains, stomach-dropping ascents and descents, and incomparable vistas, biblical theology is like a powerful sportscar and Alex Duke is a great driver: fearless, capable, and fun. Buckle up. This is going to be good.

What can you expect from the ride? Big truths communicated clearly and an uproariously good time. Alex Duke can really write. I can think of only one person who imparts as much joy to those around him as Alex does, and that guy's nickname is Doc Fun. When was the last time you laughed out loud while reading a serious analysis of an ancient text? And with the surprises that make you laugh, you'll also have the opportunity to understand and embrace the perspective from which Moses wrote the Torah.

If you want to learn the book of Genesis and have fun doing it, this is the book for you. There are many interpretations in it, so you should be a Berean, searching the Scriptures to see whether these things are so (Acts 17:11). This book will make you laugh, but it will also make you think, sending you back to the Bible to read with new questions, new insights, and new ways of processing the great story Moses tells in Genesis.

This isn't a book about writing, but if you want to be a better writer, you should read this book. Pay attention to the pacing, the surprise, the way every word has to be just right to achieve its effects: causing insight, imparting joy, and evoking laughter.[1] Notice the comfort Alex feels in his own skin. Ask yourself where it comes from and how he does it. What words did he eliminate to make that phrase prompt your belly laugh? Where does he get these crazy but apt illustrations? How does he communicate genuine humility and love for people in a way that surprises and delights? Part of the answer is that he really is humble, he really does love, and he really is paying attention. Alex is a man of character, a Christlike man, and his virtue flows out of his experience of God and his understanding of the Scriptures. Go and imitate his faith and godliness. Pay close attention to the Bible. Sponge up all of it you can. Love God and his people, the gospel and the church, then do what Alex does: let it rip for the glory of God.

Martin Luther said to love God and do as you please. Alex has captured that spirit in this book. He loves the Lord, loves the Word, loves God's people, and he's clearly enjoying being behind the wheel of a fabulous car on an epic drive. Enjoy the ride with him in this book, and we'd love to have you continue the journey with us on the *BibleTalk* podcast (www.9marks.org/podcast/bible-talk/).

—**JAMES M. HAMILTON JR.**, professor of biblical theology, The Southern Baptist Theological Seminary

---

1. As I read, I actually began to look forward to the footnotes. When I think of authors able to write entertaining footnotes, Andrew Peterson comes to mind. You never know what you're going to get, and so you start to anticipate the next one. When was the last time you felt that way about footnotes?

PREFACE TO THE 9MARKS SERIES

The 9Marks series of books is premised on two basic ideas.

First, the local church is far more important to the Christian life than many Christians today perhaps realize.

Second, local churches grow in life and vitality as they organize their lives around God's Word. God speaks. Churches should listen and follow. It's that simple. When a church listens and follows, it begins to look like the one it is following. It reflects his love and holiness. It displays his glory. A church will look like him as it listens to him.

So our basic message to churches is, don't look to the best business practices or the latest styles; look to God. Start by listening to God's Word again.

Out of this overall project comes the 9Marks series of books. Some target pastors. Some target church members. Hopefully all will combine careful biblical examination, theological reflection, cultural consideration, corporate application, and even a bit of individual exhortation. The best Christian books are always both theological and practical. You can find the entire list at 9Marks.org.

It is our prayer that God will use this volume and the others to help prepare his bride, the church, with radiance and splendor for the day of his coming.

AN ATTEMPT TO EXPLAIN WHAT EXACTLY WE'RE DOING HERE

One of the many joys of student ministry is getting credit for just showing up at things—junior-varsity wrestling matches, choir concerts, archery tournaments, volleyball games, a version of *The Pilgrim's Progress* put on by the homeschool co-op that meets at a tiny Baptist church, a version of *Anastasia* put on by the massive public school in its few-thousand person "theater center." I've told my students I'll go anywhere except a cross-country meet. I can't spend my Saturday mornings waiting for a student to run near me for a few seconds, lacking the lactic acid even to wave hello.

But so far, nothing compares to the experience of middle-school basketball. It's not merely chaotic, it is chaos itself. Its pace is glacial, its structure gelatinous. The court is too long, the rim is too high, the players are too short, the jump balls are too innumerable, and the referees are downright puritanical. The rebounds are more received than achieved. The occasional bursts of shotmaking success—when a midrange heave or a maniacal lay-up manages to tumble through the net—don't last long. Turnovers beget turnovers beget turnovers as tears and slumped shoulders fill the bench. I'm reminded of the apostle Paul's words, "For I do not understand my own actions. For I do not do what I want, but I do the very thing I hate" (Rom. 7:15 ESV). *That's* middle-school basketball.

And I get credit just for showing up!

THE CHAOS OF READING YOUR BIBLE

Many Christians open their Bibles and find themselves looking at the equivalent of a middle-school basketball game. The pace and structure don't make any sense. Sometimes the pace is glacially slow, and other times it's too fast. Sometimes the text is repetitive and obsessed with weird details; other times it seemingly skips right over the important stuff. The books are too long, the situations and characters are too unrelatable, the sins are too grievous, and—if we're being honest—sometimes God himself seems a bit puritanical. The whole thing is just so chaotic.

But we keep reading. Why? Because we know we get credit just for showing up. And, well, that's kind of true! We cannot love or understand something we ignore, so we are wise to keep putting God's words before our eyes (cf. Ps. 119:97–104).

I realize the comparison between bumbling middle-school basketball players and eager Bible readers may come across as condescending. It's not. I promise I'm not describing you. I'm describing me.

THE GOAL OF THIS BOOK

I'm just an ordinary guy who has sat at the feet of some wonderful teachers who have taught him the Bible. Yes, I went to seminary, but I got a D minus in Hebrew. I can't discern the difference between a Hebrew character and a Rorschach test.

And yet I'm living proof that the Bible can be understood and enjoyed by ordinary people. Let me up the ante a bit: the Bible can be understood and enjoyed *in detail* by ordinary people. Yes, it takes some work, and yes, it really helps to learn from those who have given their lives to serious study of the Scriptures in their original languages. But you can open your Bible, even to its most perplexing parts, and profit. You can make progress in learning how to discern a passage's structure and meaning. You can begin to see that Old Testament characters aren't mere trampolines to Jesus but full and complex human beings whose hopes and fears aren't all that different from your own.

You don't need a seminary degree or a high IQ to understand Genesis. You simply need to learn how to be a careful reader of the Scriptures. Moses isn't an idiot.[1] He's not just writing riffraff to fill the Holy Spirit's inflexible word count. He's telling a story to his friends who are wandering in the wilderness and waiting to get home. He loves them and wants to encourage them.

So much in the book of Genesis vexes us. Sure, we understand the stories on a basic sentence level, but we don't know how they connect to the whole. Why does he spend so much time on Abraham haggling with a random Hittite about a dingy cave? Why do so many people keep sleeping around with or trying to murder their own family? Why do we wait for the reunion between Jacob and Joseph for almost ten chapters only to rush through it and end the scene with Jacob saying, "Now I am ready to die"?

We have so many questions. But let's not get ahead of ourselves.

HOW TO READ THIS BOOK

Before we get started, let's walk through some basic instructions. Unlike the Holy Spirit, my benevolent editors at Zondervan *have* given me a word count. So for me, that means I can't just be out here copying

---

1. Yes, Moses wrote the Torah, including Genesis. Jesus believed it, so I do too (John 5:46–47; Luke 24:27).

and pasting large chunks of Scripture willy-nilly. For you, that means you should read this book with a Bible open or at least nearby.

Each chapter is devoted to a chunk of text. For example, chapter 1 covers Genesis 1–2. Chapter 15 covers Genesis 46–50. These chapters are then broken down into subsections. For example: "Genesis 2:4–25 // At Last!" That's a fun one. My advice to you is simple: read the Scripture portion in Genesis before you read the corresponding subsection in the book. Moses first, then me. Moses first, then me. Got it?

A FEW CLARIFYING COMMENTS

I can imagine people reading this book and having more questions for me than for Moses. Why doesn't Alex talk about the New Testament more? Why doesn't he spend more time on how many of these characters and events are fulfilled in Jesus? I could imagine another group of people wondering why there's not more application. Does the book of Genesis have nothing to help me live my life today? I am sympathetic to these hypothetical questions. But let me briefly explain myself.

What follows is not a bunch of sermonettes that end every section by rushing to Jesus. What follows is not full of moral lessons that we can—and should!—take away from the characters we'll come across. It's also not a technical commentary that tells us where modern-day Beersheba is or implies that we need to be familiar with a bunch of academic jargon to understand what's going on. I'm thankful for such books—for sermons, for moral lessons, even for technical commentaries—but this book means to be a little bit different.

From Eden to Egypt simply is, as the subtitle suggests, a guided tour. As we walk slowly through the story of Genesis, I'll explain what we're looking at. There's humor and sorrow in this book. There's life and death in this book. There's salvation and judgment in this book. It really is a masterpiece, and we should try our best to understand what Moses is doing on his own terms. That's the main goal. Yes, we'll sometimes talk about how to connect what we're reading to Jesus. After all, Jesus showed those weary travelers on the road to Emmaus that Moses means for Genesis to pave the way for the Messiah (Luke 24:27). And yes, we'll apply what we're reading to our lives today. After all, Paul says Israel's history was written down as a warning to those of us lucky enough to read it (1 Cor. 10:11). But those are both secondary pursuits.

BEFORE WE BEGIN, AN EXISTENTIAL CRISIS

The first rule of joining the author club is that you tell people you're about to join the author club. You tell people you're writing a book.

"How's your day going?"

"It's going okay, thanks for asking. I'm writing a book."

"Did you see the game last night?"

"The game? Oh, yeah, I watched it . . . while I was writing a book."

"What do you want for dinner?"

"I'm writing a book."

Most people are usually kind, so when they hear such non sequiturs, they usually respond with a compliment and a sincere question: "Oh, really, how cool! What's it about?" Just FYI, there's no worse question you could possibly ask someone who's about to join the author club. Though the question sounds harmless, it actually has fangs and eyes and can read our minds. It shreds our confidence and peers into our souls. It feels unanswerable, inscrutable, devilish, divine. How detailed should I be without sounding like a pompous idiot? All this internal processing feels like it's happening in slow-motion hyperspeed. The hesitation makes us wonder: *If they don't want to listen to my answer now, then why would anyone ever want to read a single syllable I ever write?*

Eventually, though, I found an answer that didn't make me want to melt into the center of the earth.

"I'm writing a book about Genesis for normal people."

I hope it helps. Now let's get started.

HANG ON, BEFORE WE START, A BRIEF BUT NECESSARY ATTEMPT TO EXPLAIN HOW EXACTLY THIS BOOK CAME TO BE

> The events depicted in this film took place in Minnesota in 1987. At the request of the survivors, the names have been changed. Out of respect for the dead, the rest has been told exactly as it occurred.
>
> —*FARGO* (1996)

Forgive all the throat-clearing, but there's just one more thing I have to tell you: this book wouldn't exist without Sam Emadi and Jim Hamilton.

Since 2014, I've worked for a ministry called 9Marks. On September 9, 2020, we started a podcast called *Bible Talk*.[1] The goal was simple: to talk about the Bible. Episode 1 covered Genesis 1:1–3:19;

---

1. Available wherever you listen to podcasts.

it was titled "On the Serpent, the Promised Seed, and Nahash the King of the Ammonites." Just last week, we recorded an episode on 1 Kings 10; it was titled "On the Queen of Sheba Losing Her Breath at Solomon's Blessed Reign and Burgeoning Roth IRA." For 121 episodes now, we've had a good time. I can't believe I get to do this for a living. What a gift.

At the beginning of every episode, I start by saying, "Welcome to Episode ___ of *Bible Talk*, a podcast brought to you by 9Marks. 9Marks exists to . . . [blah, blah, blah]. My name is Alex Duke and with me are my two friends." And then they each say their name: "Sam Emadi." "Jim Hamilton." It takes several hours before you can begin to tell their voices apart.

I'm the host of *Bible Talk*. I'm the everyman, the one whose aw-shucks curiosity is supposed to make our occasionally complex conversations enjoyable for "normal people." Jim and Sam are the experts. They both have PhDs. Sam is younger, a newish pastor. He studied under Jim, who's both a pastor and a seminary professor. Sam's dissertation got published, and I heard through the grapevine that it's extremely, extremely good. It's on the Joseph story. Jim has forgotten how many books he's written. They're all under his scholarly sobriquet: James M. Hamilton.[2] His productivity is awe inspiring.

Apart from one book of Jim's that I had to read in seminary, I have not read any of their books. But I have talked to them about the Bible for dozens and dozens and dozens of hours. These weekly conversations are among my life's greatest joys. Their attentiveness to the Word has shaped my understanding and sharpened my instincts. They've doublehandedly changed the way I read the Bible. Of course, there are times when I don't know what they're talking about. In these moments, I nod my head slowly and say something like, "Huh, interesting." But most of the time, when I'm silent, it's because I'm in awe of how God's Word is starting to

---

2. That would be like if someone named "E. A. Duke" wrote this book. (I could hardly type that name without laughing.)

both click and expand in my mind and heart. It's beautiful. These men have changed the way I parent and pastor and preach.

Okay, so what's all this have to do with *From Eden to Egypt*? It's probably most accurate to say that this book is inspired by the first twenty episodes of *Bible Talk*. That's how long it took us to get through Genesis. To be clear, I didn't merely transcribe our conversations from podcast to page. But they were my starting point, and they shaped my writing in profound ways.

There was a season when this book was going to be authored by all three of us: Alex Duke, James M. Hamilton, and Samuel C. Emadi. Then there was a season when it was going to be authored by Alex Duke *with* James M. Hamilton and Samuel C. Emadi. And then, when it became clear that I'd do most of the work, there was still another season when it was going to be authored by Alex Duke with James M. Hamilton and Samuel C. Emadi. Well, flip to the cover and you'll see how all that ended up.

The Coen Brothers' tragicomic *Fargo* begins with the title card given in the epigraph at the beginning of this section. Jim and Sam didn't request to have their names removed; after all, they haven't even read it (yet)! But as I got farther and farther along, I realized my chapters had become less and less "exactly as they occurred" on *Bible Talk*.

And so *From Eden to Egypt* is simply by me, Alex Duke.

Since I'm eager to avoid a Christopher Marlowe–William Shakespeare or Truman Capote–Harper Lee situation, I am delighted to give credit where credit is due. Sometimes, in our conversations, Jim and Sam would phrase things so beautifully and succinctly that I simply chose to borrow their words for this book. When that happens, I've footnoted the overlap. I suppose there could be situations in which their wisdom has so indelibly attached itself to my brain that it's now disguised as my own. If any intrepid reader discovers such discrepancies, I promise they are accidental, and I apologize.

For the most part, when you find Jim's or Sam's name in the footnotes, it's because I want to draw your attention to something they said in an episode of *Bible Talk*. This book is just barely longer than 65,000 words. As a guided tour, it's meant to offer familiarity, not expertise. We've barely scratched the surface of Moses' masterpiece. So consider these footnotes invitations to deeper conversations.

When you discover flaws or foolishness or fumbled attempts at humor, the fault is entirely mine. When you discover insight or clarity, the fruit is likely theirs. To repeat what I said at the beginning, this book wouldn't exist without Sam Emadi and Jim Hamilton, my two friends.

Okay, *now* let's get started.

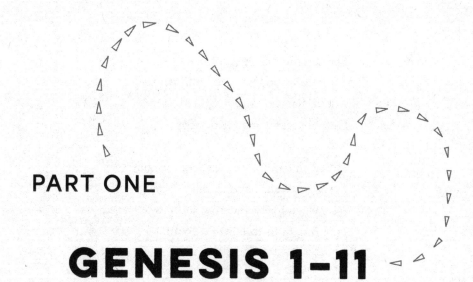

PART ONE

GENESIS 1-11

Before Jehovah's awful throne,
Ye nations, bow with sacred joy;
Know that the Lord is God alone;
He can create, and He destroy.

His sovereign power, without our aid,
Made us of clay, and formed us men;
And when like wandering sheep we strayed,
He brought us to His fold again.

We are His people, we His care,
Our souls, and all our mortal frame;
What lasting honors shall we rear,
Almighty Maker, to Thy name.

We'll crowd Thy gates with thankful songs,
High as the heavens our voices raise;
And earth, with her ten thousand tongues,
Shall fill Thy courts with sounding praise.

Wide as the world is Thy command,
Vast as eternity Thy love;
Firm as a rock Thy truth must stand,
When rolling years shall cease to move.

–ISAAC WATTS, "BEFORE JEHOVAH'S AWFUL THRONE"

We have to go back.

–JACK, *LOST*

ONE

GENESIS 1-2

The first monster, Bloodletter, ripped off their heads. Gouger of Faces plucked out their eyeballs and Crunching Jaguar and Tearing Jaguar ripped off the people's limbs and then ate them.

–*THE POPOL VUH,* A MAYAN CREATION MYTH

You complete me.

–JERRY, *JERRY MAGUIRE*

I told you already my thoughts on middle-school basketball: it's chaos marked by bursts of frustrated success. In at least this sense, many of history's creation narratives resemble middle-school basketball: chaos marked by bursts of frustrated success. Gods bloody and bruise one another as they give birth to existence.

A few examples. First, there's Babylon's *Enuma Elish.* Here's the conclusion: "After killing Tiamat, Marduk splits her body in two, making one half the sky and one half the earth. He makes humans from his own flesh and bone and brings order to the universe." In Babylon, existence erupts in the aftermath of a divine domestic dispute, and human beings are then cobbled together by the bloody champion's flesh and bone.

The *Popol Vuh*, quoted in the epigraph to this chapter, is the Mayans' oral tradition of creation, and it is, in a word, *wild*. You could say it takes my middle-school basketball comparison a bit too far because it features the lord of the underworld decapitating someone and using their head during a game of something called Maya Ball. Here's a summary: "By tradition, the twin brothers Hun Hunaphu and Xbalanque used their time on earth to play ball. . . . [T]he noise of the game aroused the anger of Vucub Came, the master of the underworld. A fight ensued, which resulted in the formation of the game. After the game, one of the brothers was decapitated and his head was used as the game ball."[1]

Yikes!

This creation myth goes on to describe how the Mayan gods created humans the way Thomas Edison created lightbulbs—by trial and error. First they tried earth and mud. It failed. Then they tried wood. It also failed. The earth-and-mud men were droopy and dissolvable. The wooden men were sturdy—an improvement!—but also dumb and clumsy.[2] (Apologies to Pinocchio and his loved ones.) In Maya, existence erupts in fits and starts, and human beings are the bloody result of a few bloodthirsty gods' experiments with existence.

GENESIS 1:1–2:3 // GOD'S VERY GOOD WORLD, OUR VERY SPECIAL JOB

Genesis 1–2 isn't in direct conversation with these stories.[3] But remember: their author, Moses, grew up in Egypt. His audience did, too.

---

1. Yes, I found this on Wikipedia: https://en.wikipedia.org/wiki/Maya_Ballgame.
2. If you're curious, the epigraph to this chapter summarizes how the frustrated gods sent monsters to kill one of their failed attempts at humanity so they could start over.
3. Moses wrote Genesis sometime after the exodus in 1446 BCE, and the rest of the Torah sometime before he died. The *Enuma Elish* is dated around 1200 BCE, though it could have

They'd heard the Egyptian counter-creation myths. These were less bloody but nonetheless explained humanity as the fruit of chaos, the heavens and the earth as the culmination of divine opposition. Hopefully you've done your homework and read Genesis 1–2. If you have, you'll see that the contrasts between these accounts and the Bible's are striking.

Let's talk about a few.

First, God has no rival. From the Scriptures' first syllable, it's clear: the real God who really exists is entirely standalone and sovereign. He doesn't share the sky. He has no divine roommate, no heavenly henchmen, no cosmic consigliere. He is supreme. Nothing predates him; no one pesters him.

Moses begins, "In the beginning, God created the heavens and the earth." He doesn't bury the lede. He starts with the bottom line up-front: God did everything by himself.

Now notice what comes next: a formless void and a dark deep (1:2). These images are enigmatic. Our minds can't picture what a formless and void earth is, much less what it looks like. That's okay. That's not the point. The point is that before the beginning of creation, there was God and only God. God, and God alone, brought something out of nothing, form to the formlessness, shape to the void, light to the darkness.

Who lit the fire of a thousand burning suns?[4] No one but God. What preexisting material did he use? Nothing. He doesn't need primordial ooze or a match and a spark or the entrails of his enemies. He needs nothing outside of himself because all the power he needs to create everything resides in himself. God needed nothing to create everything.

He has no rival.

---

existed in various forms around the same time as the Torah. The *Popol Vuh* began as an oral tradition, as all these stories did, but since it came from the other side of the world and wasn't written down until much later, its history remains difficult to trace.

4. Sovereign Grace, "He Is Our God."

Second, God's creation is the fruit of wisdom, not war. I once read something that said if earth were 1 percent closer to the sun, we would all burn to a crisp, and if we were 1 percent farther away, we would all freeze to death. Some might hear that and think, "Wow, we are so lucky!" I hear it and think, "Wow, God is so wise."

As Moses walks through the days of creation, he revels in God's wisdom. I'm far from the first to notice this pattern, but it's worth restating:

	Day 1		**Day 4**
	Light and dark		Sun, moon, and stars
	Day 2		**Day 5**
	Sea and sky		Fish and birds
	Day 3		**Day 6**
	Dry land		Land animals and man

In days 1–3, God designs the architecture of the universe, the blueprint for life as we know it. In days 4–6, he picks out the furniture and fills out the rooms he's already formed.

It might be tempting to ask gotcha questions like, "Hold up! How was there 'evening and morning' when the sun, moon, and stars weren't even created until day 4?" Clever question, but ultimately irrelevant.[5] Moses isn't your middle-school science teacher, and Genesis 1 isn't a chapter from your textbook. Gensis 1 is the beginning of Moses' history of God's people, and Genesis 1–2 reveals that their Creator and King is orderly and wise, not chaotic and cantankerous. Everything in God's creation is fit for flourishing. He didn't spin the dreidel and walk away. He created the world to care for the world—from red dwarfs to red herrings to red algae to redheads.

---

5. I'd say the same to those who approach Genesis 1 as if Moses offers definitive answers on the age of the universe. Treating Genesis this way is like looking to Leviticus' list of clean and unclean animals as a diet plan; there might be some wisdom there, but it's not the story Moses is telling.

All this can be summed up in a single word: it's "good." That's how God repeatedly assesses his work (1:10, 12, 18, 21, 25, 31). This adjective might seem meager, especially for those of us with kids who use it *ad nauseam*. ("How was your day, honey?" "Good." "How was soccer practice?" "Good.") But when God calls his work good, we shouldn't hear faint praise. We should crane our necks and listen for thunderous applause. Why? Because at the beginning of the beginning, everything is fit for flourishing—from the parts to the whole. Everything is good.

God's creation is the fruit of wisdom, not war. And then it gets better.

Third, human beings aren't trial-and-error curiosities. They're the crown jewel of creation. By the time we get to 1:26, the repetition stops and Moses slows down for the climax of his narrative, the creation of humanity. In this passage, we receive two things from our Creator: a special status and a special job (1:26–27).

The special status? We're made in God's image. That's one of those phrases Christians say a lot and we all just kind of assume we know what it means. Humans are "made in the image of God," and that's why we're rational beings. Or that's why we communicate with more than barks and meows. Or that's why we're so good at art and music and cooking compared with, like, grizzly bears or orangutans. But those conclusions aren't saying the same things. So what does it actually mean to be made in the image of God?

Let me get right to it: our special status means we have both the ability and the obligation to do our special job. What's our special job? The Lord tells us right here. We are to be fruitful and multiply in order to fill the earth and subdue it. To have, in a word, dominion (1:26, 28). To rule and to reflect our Creator.

Our creation in the image of God means we uniquely reflect our Creator to the rest of creation. Does this mean human beings are derivative deities or "little gods"? Not at all. God inhabits the divine class all by himself. We are the crown jewel of the class of creation. The Lord alone is Creator, and we are stewards of a subset of his creation (1:28).

I wonder if you ever noticed that our authority is hemmed in: "Rule over the fish in the sea and the birds in the sky and over every living creature that moves on the ground" (1:28). It stops at the sea and the sky. But God's? His is universal, unlimited, all encompassing. It's total and complete. I also wonder if you noticed that he has to *give* dominion and we have to *receive* it (1:28). Apart from God's generous initiative, it wouldn't be ours. Nothing would be ours! Genesis 1 teaches us we can't do anything without God's authorization. We can't have dominion and subdue the earth without God telling us to. We can't eat kumquats or kiwis or pears or peaches (1:29–30) without God telling us to. This is what it means to be a steward, not a sovereign. We're not in charge.[6] And yet, unbelievably, we're given the blessed (1:22, 28) job to reflect him to the rest of creation.

Think about it. This is how the Lord has set up his universe: he wants human beings to fill the earth as mini mirrors of their Creator. This is so important to him, so vital to his creative endeavor, that it's not until he creates and commissions us that he stands back and upgrades his assessment from "good" to "very good" (v. 31). William Shakespeare is right: all the world's a stage.[7] But it's not a stage for men to muse on the life cycle of men, Elizabethan or otherwise. It's a stage for men to mimic their God.

No other creatures enjoy such a high calling. So when we read Genesis 1, we should be astounded at God's power and wisdom. Indeed. But we should also be astounded at what it means to be a *you*, a male or female created in his image. We're not a bag of bones and blood. We're not a supercomputer with feelings. We're the very good jewel in King Creator's crown. We reflect him as we exercise our rule over the raw materials of this world, as we put the orderliness of God's wise world to work by working hard and making useful and beautiful

---

6. If you've ever wondered why God put an untouchable tree in the garden in the first place, now you have your answer. Adam is the height of creation, sure, but he's not the king of creation. His job to rule is legitimate, but not ultimate. Thanks to my pastor Greg Gilbert for this insight.

7. William Shakespeare, *As You Like It*, act 2, scene 7.

things. Whether you're a middle-school lifeguard or a middle-aged CEO or a mom at home with three little kids, we all have a job to do and a special status that enables us to do it. What a blessing.

GENESIS 2:4-25 // "AT LAST!"

When we first read Genesis 2:4, it's tempting to do a double take. *Wait a second, didn't we just cover this!* Sort of, but not exactly. Think of Genesis 1 as a picture of your family tree. It accurately records with some remove the order of events that led to your existence. Think of Genesis 2 as sitting down with your grandparents and asking them about their wedding day. This is a zoomed-in version of the same story, not the second creation of a second man. But rather than offer a poetic and chronological report, Moses rewinds the tape on certain events of Genesis 1.

Suddenly, day 3's dry land has a name: "a garden in Eden" (2:8 ESV). Day 2's sea is now a river, and then four rivers with four names: Pishon, Gihon, Tigris, and Euphrates (2:10–14).[8] Day 6's man is not merely created but formed "of dust from the ground" as God "breathed into his nostrils the breath of life" (2:7). This man has the same gig: work and keep the garden (2:15).[9] But something's not quite right. After the chorus of good-good-good-good-good-very good in Genesis 1, the Lord's assessment in Genesis 2:18 is like a cat's claws on a chalkboard: "It is not good that the man should be alone" (ESV). We have a problem. What's the solution? A helper (2:18, 20). But who?

When I was seven, my Christmas list—for Santa, for my

---

8. You might be thinking, "Um, gardens aren't dry and seas aren't rivers." You'd be right! But look back to how Moses uses those phrases. Dry land (1:10) simply means "not sea," and sea simply refers to "not sky" or all water (1:9). With this in mind, a garden and four rivers does in fact specify what kind of dry land and sea we're dealing with. It's not a contradiction but a closeup.

9. "Work it and keep it" offers us a clue that Moses wants us to see that Eden is a kind of temple, where God dwells with his people. How do we know? Because Moses tells us that priests work and keep the temple (Num. 1:53).

grandparents, for my parents, for anyone who could read—featured one item: a golden retriever named Chloe. When Christmas came, I ran downstairs and saw a bunch of small gifts with my name on the wrapping paper. One by one, I ripped them open: a collar, a chew toy, a bone, a leash. But no dog. After I opened the final gift—a dog bowl, for crying out loud—I was wracked with confusion and bubbling with frustration. Was this some kind of cruel joke? Why was everyone so smirky? Could I survive if I ran away? Then my brother darted upstairs and came down with something furry in his arms: a golden retriever named Chloe.

At last!

I imagine the man in the garden felt a lot like me on that Christmas morning. The Lord paraded in front of him a host of unfit gifts—an ant, an antelope, a toucan, a tamarin. The delayed relief heightens the anticipation. No, no, no, no, no. From aardvark to zebra, it's a no. And then the Lord makes from Adam's rib a woman, finally a helper "fit" for him, and the man channels his inner Etta James and begins to sing. "At last!" (2:23 ESV).

Remember, Genesis 2 is like talking to your grandparents about their wedding day. So where's the wedding? It's right here. Did you see it? Moses frames the creation of Eve as both a birth and a marriage. So much so that he breaks genre for a verse and makes an argument reflecting on the story he has just told. Look again at 2:24 in the ESV. That word "therefore" signals a brief shift from narration to discourse, from plot to principle. It's as if he's saying, "Look, the Lord created Adam and Eve to set up a paradigm not merely for males and females in general but for husbands and wives in particular." By the end of Genesis 2, we realize that Moses has been writing both a creation story and a marriage story all along. Though Adam had no father and mother to leave, he did now have a wife to hold fast to.

Genesis 2 double-clicks on Genesis 1:26–31 and fills in some missing information. As it turns out, the creation story of Genesis 1 had some drama in it: we didn't go straight from good to very good, but we went from good (1:25) to not good (2:18) to very good (1:31). Before sin even enters the world, the Lord is fixing our problems and giving us what we need.

As we arrive at the end of Moses' beginning, what have we learned?

- The Lord has no rival.
- His creation is wise and orderly.
- The peak of this creation is humanity—you and me.
- Humans have a special status (created in the image of God) that gives us the ability and obligation to do our special job (to subdue the earth as we mirror God to the rest of creation).[10]
- The creation of Eve is also the creation of marriage.

Genesis 2 ends with Adam and Eve on their honeymoon. They are husband and wife in a world without the memory of sin and any experience of shame. It's beautiful. It's unbelievable. It makes us long for something similar.

But no honeymoon lasts forever.

---

10. Did you notice who names the animals? It's not the Lord, it's the man. He's already exerting his authority over the rest of creation.

TWO

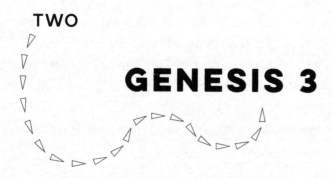

GENESIS 3

Snakes, why did it have to be snakes?

—INDIANA JONES, *RAIDERS OF THE LOST ARK*

Don't get me wrong when I tell you that Tom, while being a very nice guy, is the devil. . . . What do you think the devil is going to look like if he's around? . . . C'mon! Nobody is going to be taken in by a guy with a long, red, pointy tail! C'mon, what's he gonna sound like? [*hisses dramatically*] . . . No, I'm semiserious here. He will be attractive. He will be nice and helpful. He'll get a job where he influences a great, God-fearing nation. He'll never do any evil thing, never deliberately hurt a living thing. He'll just bit by little bit lower our standards where they are important. Just a tiny little bit. Just coax along—flash over substance! Just a tiny little bit. And he'll talk about all of us really being salesmen. And he'll get all the great women.

—AARON ALTMAN, *BROADCAST NEWS*

We left Genesis 1–2 in a picturesque paradise. In it were two people, a husband and a wife, who were naked and without shame. They lived there, walking and talking with God, and it was good. We now arrive at Genesis 3, in which Moses explains how sin crashes into creation and then proceeds to ruin everything and everyone. And yet we'll also see a spark of God's promise about how he will—one day—clean this whole mess up by finally crushing the head of the serpent, Satan's mouthpiece.[1]

Let's look more closely at this chapter, which plays out like a tragic, five-act origin story for original sin.

ACT 1: MOTIVE AND OPPORTUNITY (3:1-5)

Genesis 1–2 celebrates God's creativity and generosity. He didn't just make a photosynthesis device and blithely call it Tree 1. No, he created "all kinds of trees . . . that were pleasing to the eye and good for food" (2:9). Why the beauty and variety? Because God is creative. Why the food? Because God is generous. The garden of Eden was the perfect place for a honeymoon, an all-inclusive resort with a single exclusion: the tree of the knowledge of good and evil. If you eat from that tree, the Lord said, you'll die. You'll find not protein but poison (2:16–17).[2]

Notice how the serpent begins his attack with a bad-faith question: Did God *really* say you can't have any of this stuff? Eve swats it away at first (3:2), but she should have stopped talking sooner because what ultimately comes out of her mouth is both confident and imprecise.

---

1. We know the serpent is Satan because of passages like John 8:44 and Rev. 12:9. We don't know much about Satan's origin story except that he was an angel who rebelled in heaven. As a result, God threw him down to earth, where he spent the rest of his days making war against the seed of the woman. Check out Rev. 12:7–17 for the clearest passage on this, and pay special attention to how that passage interacts with the upcoming curses at the end of Genesis 3.

2. Remember this formula: obedience to God's word leads to life. Disobedience leads to death. It's a repeated refrain throughout the Torah and really the entire Bible.

If you've ever talked to a college freshman, you're familiar with this dangerous mixture.

Look again at 3:3. Eve is half right and half wrong. She remembered that God gave her and Adam trees for food—except for that one in the middle of the garden, the one with the really long name she couldn't recall. She also remembered the punishment: death. So far, so good.

But then she smuggles in something new: oh, God also said we shouldn't even touch that dangerous tree! Now, this prohibition isn't a terrible idea, but it's from her, not the Lord. It's a human deduction, not a divine command. Eve's foggy knowledge leads her to add to God's revelation, which then provides an opportunity for the serpent to attack his character.

It's been a few years now, but do you remember "the slap heard 'round the world"? It happened at the 2022 Academy Awards. Comedian Chris Rock made an unseemly joke about Jada Pinkett Smith, Will Smith's wife. Within seconds, the Fresh Prince of Bel-Air walked onto the stage and socked Chris Rock in the jaw. It was one of the most shocking things I've ever seen on TV. I couldn't believe it. That's Will Smith! He's charming (*The Fresh Prince of Bel-Air*; *Hitch*) and inspiring (*The Pursuit of Happyness*). He's a hero who punches aliens (*Independence Day*) and robots (*I, Robot*) and "vampiric, albino, cannibalistic mutants called Darkseekers"[3] (*I Am Legend*). He doesn't punch humans![4]

Of course, I don't know Will Smith from Adam. In fact, I probably know Adam better. Any knowledge I have of Will Smith is essentially made up. It's marketing. He's an actor, a talented guy who fakes being other guys for money. That doesn't mean he's a horrible person. But it does mean that I don't know him and therefore shouldn't have been shocked when he coldcocked Chris Rock.

It's easy to be surprised by God's actions when we don't know his

---

3. That extremely precise descriptor is from Wikipedia.
4. Except for when he does (*Ali*).

character.[5] So how do we learn about his character? The same way as Adam and Eve: by listening to and delighting in his word. Eve had but a few sentences to listen to and delight in. But her knowledge was foggy and her delight was dim, so she was susceptible to doubt, temptation, and sin. We have *several thousand* sentences to listen to and delight in. How foggy are they to us? How dim is our delight?

The serpent seizes on Eve's inexact knowledge, which opens the door for her to doubt God's character. Look again at 3:4. The serpent's question evolves from a vague suggestion into outright opposition. "Did God really say?" becomes "God *lied* when he said." Why? Because, the serpent hisses, God will be threatened if you eat. He doesn't want you to become "like him" (3:5).

How strange. Eve should have realized the real liar was the one slithering at her feet. She should have said, "What are you talking about? My husband and I are already 'like God'! We're made in his image. Which reminds me, I have dominion over creatures like you, so I'm not going to listen to you tempt me to overthrow the creator of the universe!"

This won't be the last time you read this: Moses is a masterful storyteller. In barely two and a half chapters, he has subtly introduced the stakes of existence. Did you notice? He has sketched out the perfect order of Genesis 1–2 versus the mangled order of Genesis 3. There's God's way versus the serpent's way; there's obedience and life versus sin and death.

- God's way: God creates man to have dominion over creatures and to listen to his word.
- Serpent's way: creatures tempt man to have dominion over God by rejecting his word.[6]

---

5. Notice how through their entire conversation (Gen. 3:1–5), the covenant name of God disappears. Moses wants us to know that though Satan seems to know "God," he certainly doesn't believe in the "Lord God." Thanks to Greg Gilbert—again—for this insight.

6. This observation is not original to me. I first heard it from my pastor, Greg Gilbert. The apostle Paul seems to pick up on this understanding of sin in Rom. 1:24–25.

What the serpent offers Eve is not merely an opportunity to indulge her desire or satisfy her curiosity. Far from it. The serpent invites Eve and the whole human race into rebellion. You might have heard sin described as "missing the mark" of God's intentions. Such a description is like describing war as "nations disagreeing"—it's technically true but embarrassingly undersells the seriousness of the situation. Sin is not missing the target despite our best efforts. Sin is high-handed rebellion against our Creator.

And as we're about to see, that means the consequences must be serious, too.

ACT 2: THE CRIME (3:6)

We're moving slowly through these opening chapters because they lay the foundation for everything to come. They answer big questions: Who created us? (God.) Are we different from animals? (Yes.) How should we relate to him? (By obeying his Word and reflecting his character through our dominion over creation.)

Verse 6 answers another big question: What's wrong with us?

The answer: we're cracked by sin.

And it all started with a gaze. Look again at 3:6 and pay attention to Moses' description. No word is wasted. Eve saw the fruit of the tree was two things: pleasing to the eye and good for food. Great start. That's exactly why God made the tree (2:9)![7] But then Moses adds another detail: Eve also saw that the fruit was desirable for "gaining wisdom" (3:6). No, Eve, no! Wisdom comes through listening to and delighting in God's word, not by taking and eating his creation. There's no wisdom in a strawberry. Strawberries are meant to be savored and digested, not studied and delighted in.

---

7. Christians ought to be the most eager to enjoy creation because when we revel in, for example, a tree's beauty or a meal's deliciousness, we are reflecting our Creator.

But Eve had convinced herself that God had withheld something she needed, that he hadn't told her the whole story. So she sinned. She rebelled against her Creator and King. And notice what happens next: she passes down her shame. She gives some fruit to her husband, who apparently doesn't care that his wife has cozied up to a lying snake.[8]

ACT 3: THE TRIAL (3:7-13)

If God didn't exist, the Bible would have taken an alternate route after Genesis 3:6. You can imagine two college freshmen who grew up in church smoking a joint for the first time. Until that moment in their dingy dorm room, they'd listened to their parents and pastors. They'd dared to resist drugs. But not anymore. So they light up—and my-oh-my that nascent buzz welcomes them into a world of shameless possibility. They sit there in wide-eyed wonder: *What else have I been missing?*

But God does exist. And so our imagination must give way to reality. Once the fruit touches their tongues, Adam and Eve are welcomed into a world of shame and separation—from each other, from their God, from the creation they're meant to care for. That's what sin really does: the scintillation lasts a few seconds, but the shame and separation stick. They used to hear God's voice and heed it, now they hear it and hide (3:8, 10).

You might be wondering to yourself, "Hang on. Why are Adam and Eve still alive? Was the serpent right?" After all, it said that when they ate the forbidden fruit, they wouldn't die but their "eyes will be opened, and [they] will be like God" (3:5). Did you notice how Moses

---

8. The fact that Moses adds the startling detail about Adam—"[he] was with her" (3:6)—helps us as readers to understand that both he and Eve share culpability. Adam failed through inaction, Eve through action. In fact, it's possible Adam had already failed in his one job to "work and keep" the garden, which probably included stomping the heads of lying, hissing snakes. Later on in the Torah, priests are told to "guard" the tabernacle from profane intruders (Num. 1:53; 3:7-8). The idea is similar: Eden is where God lives, just as the tabernacle will be where God lives. Adam as the first priest had the same responsibility as the priests after him.

describes what happens immediately after they sinned? "Then the eyes of both of them were opened." Now, if the serpent was right, we'd expect the next phrase to explain how they became like God. After all, their eyes are now opened. But Moses shows us the opposite. Adam and Eve's open eyes force them to stare at their shame and vulnerability; their open eyes force them to see that they are, in fact, not like God. What they thought would bring them to some kind of heightened divine consciousness has in fact shattered their unique connection to the divine. (Again, Moses is a masterful storyteller.)

Okay, but it's still worth asking the question. God said they would "certainly die" (2:17), so why haven't they? Well, they are dead. They've died spiritually, which is made clear by their fearful hiding from God and even more so by the end of the chapter when they are banished from his presence (3:23–24). In this case, the instrument of death isn't a guillotine, it's their guilt.

Now, if the God who really exists were like Bloodletter or Gouger of Faces,[9] then the Bible would have taken a different route yet again after Genesis 3:9. I suspect God would have extinguished Adam and Eve and started over. But instead he puts them on trial and pursues them with a series of questions:

- "Where are you?" (3:9).
- "Who told you that you were naked?" (3:11).
- "Have you eaten from the tree that I commanded you not to eat from?" (3:11).
- "What is this you have done?" (3:13).

Why does the God who knows all things ask anyone anything? It's not because he lacks evidence. He's not ignorant, he's omniscient. He asks these questions because the omniscient God to whom Adam and Eve are accountable is also the omniscient God who pursues his

---

9. See the epigraph to chapter 1.

people—even after they've messed everything up. Their sins—and ours—still have consequences. But those consequences don't cancel out God's care for his image bearers.

After Adam and Eve plead guilty (3:12–13), all that is left is for the judge of the universe to hand down his sentence.

ACT 4: THE SENTENCING (3:14-20)

Three perpetrators, three guilty verdicts, three sentences. Let's look at Adam and Eve's first, and then the serpent's.

ADAM AND EVE'S SENTENCE (3:16-20)

As one writer has ably summarized, the goal of humanity is "to be fruitful and multiply in order to fill the earth and subdue it. To have, in a word, dominion (1:26, 28)."[10] That's why God made us. Our special job is both generic and gendered—all humans have a role in each aspect, but our involvement as male and female is asymmetrical.[11] In an effort to explain what I mean, allow me to write the least controversial sentence of all time: when it comes to one aspect of our jobs, being fruitful and multiplying, men may be as necessary as women, but they certainly have the easier responsibility. I don't think I need to elaborate. Now allow me to write a more controversial sentence: when it comes to humanity's other task—having dominion over creation—both men and woman are necessary, but the involvement is asymmetrical here, too. I wouldn't say women have an easier job, but if we're following the grain of Moses' story, we notice that a man's posture is toward having dominion while a woman's is toward being fruitful and multiplying.[12]

---

10. That's me, a few pages ago.

11. Notice in Gen. 1:26–27 that the Lord doesn't say "human I created them" but "male and female I created them." To be "created male" or "created female" means something. Maleness and femaleness aren't arbitrary and meaningless. We are not all born as androgynous gatherings of cells awaiting our fundamental gender identity.

12. Forgive me in advance for such a lengthy footnote! I'm aware this sentiment could

We see this more clearly as we pay attention to the specific curses in Genesis 3. Both Adam and Eve are cursed in their dominant domains. In 3:16, the Lord curses Eve by adding pain to childbearing and rivalry to marriage. Who can say what painless childbearing would have been like? Sadly, no mother. Who can say what a conflict-free marriage would have been like? Sadly, no husband or wife. But before Genesis 3, these would have been as natural as the sun at noon. Suddenly, Eve's commission to be fruitful and fill the earth is more complicated, her obedience more difficult. The same is true for Adam. In 3:17–19, God curses him by cursing the ground with thorns and thistles.[13] Suddenly, his commission to subdue the earth by having dominion is more complicated, his obedience more difficult.[14]

---

be mangled and misappropriated. So allow these comments by Alastair Roberts to flesh it out with more nuance: "Men and women are created for different primary purposes. These purposes, when pursued in unity and with mutual support, can reflect God's own form of creative rule in the world. The man's vocation, as described in Genesis 2, primarily corresponds to the tasks of the first three days of creation: to naming, taming, dividing, and ruling. The woman's vocation, by contrast, principally involves filling, glorifying, generating, establishing communion, and bringing forth new life—all tasks associated with the second three days of creation. The differences between men and women aren't merely incidental, but integral to our purpose. They're also deeply meaningful, relating to God's own fundamental patterns of operation. God created us to be male and female and thereby to reflect his own creative rule in his world. . . .

"Humanity's varying creational vocations in Genesis don't represent the full measure or scope of men and women's callings—as if women only existed to bear children, and men only to be farmers. Rather, they're the seeds from which broader callings can thematically develop. Each man and woman must find ways to bring their gendered aptitudes, capacities, and selves that God created them with to bear upon the situations he has placed them within. Although our callings' center of gravity differs, man and woman are to work together and assist each other, each employing their particular strengths to perform humanity's common task. Neither can fulfill their vocation alone. . . .

"Expressing sexual difference in a vast array of culturally conjugated ways can display the *beauty* of our particular differences. Our differences are more than merely random and unstable assortments of contrasts between two classes of persons. Far from it. Our differences are musical and meaningful, inseparably intertwined." (Alastair Roberts, "Man and Woman in Creation (Genesis 1 and 2)," 9Marks, December 10, 2019, www.9marks.org/article/man-and -woman-in-creation-genesis-1-and-2/.

13. I've never worked on a farm a day in my life. But I have faced twenty-first-century thorns and thistles: grease fires at McDonald's, emails stuck in spam, and people (Sam Emadi) forgetting the memory card while recording a podcast.

14. We need to be careful about drawing too many direct implications from this passage, because we are, after all, in a narrative. The plot doesn't answer every question the principle might raise. For example, "Does Genesis 1–3 teach that women can't be president or that there should never be such a thing as a stay-at-home dad?" Sometimes, Moses shifts from narrative

I suspect Adam and Eve heard these curses with mixed feelings. Partly with glad relief because life would carry on through her womb and his work. Partly with guilty remorse because death is coming, just as God promised. You will eat of the dust's fruit, the Lord essentially says, until you become the dust's food.

THE SERPENT'S SENTENCE (3:14-15)

Finally, God curses the serpent above all creation by forever placing it below all creation. For trying to climb the throne of heaven, the King of Heaven condemns the serpent to the dusty ground (3:14).

We should linger on 3:15 because it's a surprising and significant verse. It's surprising because it contains breaking news: Adam and Eve will bear offspring. The death God decreed didn't mean the end of the human experiment. It's significant because it describes the conflict at the heart of our continued existence: the seed of the woman versus the seed of the serpent.

Does this mean we're about to get a bunch of stories about human heroes crushing some cobras? No. Is *Indiana Jones and the Raiders of the Lost Ark* based on a true story? Also—and unfortunately—no. The heart of this conflict has nothing to do with skin versus scales and everything to do with trusting God versus rejecting God. Through God's curse of the serpent, Moses reiterates the stakes of existence. Those who disdain God's Word and decide to live their own way prove to be offspring of the serpent. But those who align with God's purposes prove to be offspring of Eve. Though Eve is the mother of all the living (3:20), not all are her offspring in this sense. Throughout Genesis, we'll meet some sons and daughters of Eve who are more like the serpent than their mother.

At the end of 3:15, the Lord makes a prediction that will reverberate throughout the rest of Scripture. It would be simplistic to say that

---

to discourse and does the deducing for us, like we saw in Gen. 2:24. But not here. We should be careful about over-reading passages like these, even as we should be careful not to ignore their clearly stated principles.

all of Scripture is about this. And yet it would be shortsighted to ignore how vital this promise is to its main storyline.

You might be thinking, "Um, isn't the Bible ultimately about Jesus?" Yes, of course. And it's here that he first shows up. Look again at the final line of God's verdict: "He will crush your head, and you will strike his heel." Who's the "he"? Well, in Moses' mind, it's probably a bit foggy. He's recording this prophetic curse because it had been passed down through generations. He knows the Lord said it. More than that, Moses believes that one day a particular seed of the woman will crush the Enemy's head, even if in the process his heel is bruised.

Who could have imagined that God was talking about himself here? Who could have imagined God would deal death its deathblow through the death and resurrection of his Son?[15] As we read through Scripture, we find our fair share of head crushers: Moses, Jael, David, and more.[16] But all of these temporary heroes eventually get swallowed up by death. Though they strike the serpent's head, the curse of sin still crushes them. Until Jesus shows up. He's temporarily swallowed up by death before he swallows death up in victory—and then spits it out when he walks out of the grave.

The first spark of the gospel shows up in Genesis 3:15. The bad news for the serpent is good news for us. His curse is our blessing.

ACT 5: THE GRACIOUS EXILE (3:21-23)

Imagine the scene as Adam and Eve are sentenced for their sin. The Judge's final words—"And to dust you will return"—linger in the air. It's tense, somber, serious.

---

15. If you want the best chapter in the Bible to see this connection, read 1 Corinthians 15 *slowly*. A close second? Romans 5.

16. For Moses, check out how Isa. 51:9–10 describes the Lord's defeat of Rahab (the mythic, serpentine sea creature from Job 9) in terms that seem to summarize the exodus. For Jael, check out Judg. 4:16–22. For David, read 1 Samuel 17 and note that the word for Goliath's armor is the same word translated "scales." The Bible is cool.

What do you expect to happen next? If this were a true-crime documentary on Netflix, the perpetrators would stand there, slack jawed and slump shouldered, as they wordlessly contemplate their terrible fate. The judge would tap his gavel, shuffle some papers, and then disappear through the back. But here? A different scene unfolds. These perpetrators do stand silent. But this judge drops his gavel, steps down from his bench, and covers up the superficial cause of the assailants' shame.

We just talked about how Genesis 3:15 is the first step on the Bible's long road to get to Jesus. Perhaps we've already found the second step: "The LORD God made garments of skin for Adam and his wife and clothed them" (3:21). Did he use needle and thread? A sewing machine? No, he used a sacrifice. Moses' audience would have read this and immediately thought of bulls and goats and priests. And they'd have been right. The Levitical sacrificial system was their life, for it was a "reminder of sins" (Heb. 10:3). And what a gracious system it was! How else would God's people persist in God's presence? But we should read Genesis 3:21 and immediately think of Jesus. Because we know "it is impossible for the blood of bulls and goats to take away sins" (Heb. 10:4). How gracious and powerful is Jesus! Only his death can provide unfettered access to God forever.

But we're getting ahead of ourselves. Because though there are sparks of hope, Moses knows that this part of the story is a tragedy—at least for now.

Consider how much has changed since Genesis 1–2. Adam and Eve are still husband and wife, but their relationship is now marked by rivalry. They're covered up by sacrifice, but still corrupted by sin. They haven't been demoted or fired, but every bullet point of their job description has been made more difficult. This is their new reality.

And then Adam and Eve are banished from paradise. They're kicked out of their home, and the path toward the tree of life is now guarded by cherubim with a flaming sword. Is there another way in?[17]

---

17. *Whispers* Guess what? There is. The tree of life vanishes from Scripture entirely

It takes the rest of the Bible to answer that question. But for now, everything and everyone has been ruined. So we ask another question: "What's next?"

---

until its very last chapter: Revelation 22. It shows up in the new heavens and the new earth. Why? How did it get there? Because the last Adam (Jesus) obeyed, the curse is lifted for all who believe in him. As a result, God's people get to—finally!—enjoy the benefits that Adam and Eve missed out on: everlasting life and access to the presence of God. Clearly, the apostle John read Moses. When I asked my friend Nick Roark about this passage, he wrote back, "Christ's cross of wood has become a tree of life for the whole world."

Okay, one more comment that I just have to make. When Jesus died, the curtain of the temple tore in two, from top to bottom (Matt. 27:51; Mark 15:38; Luke 23:45). This of course symbolized that through Christ's death, we now all have access to God. You hopefully know that already. But did you know what the curtain of the temple had stitched all over it? Cherubim (2 Chron. 3:14). With the death of Christ, the cherubim put down their swords and welcomed God's people back into his presence. Thanks to Sam Emadi for this connection.

THREE

GENESIS 4-9

Deputy Wendell: "This is turnin' into a hell of a mess, ain't it, Sheriff?"

Sheriff Ed Tom Bell: "If it isn't, it'll do until the mess gets here."

—CORMAC MCCARTHY, *NO COUNTRY FOR OLD MEN*

We had fed the heart on fantasies,
The heart's grown brutal from the fare,
More substance in our enmities
Than in our love; oh, honey-bees
Come build in the empty house of the stare.

—W. B. YEATS, "THE STARE'S NEST BY MY WINDOW"

It's sometimes helpful to remember that not everything in your Bible is inspired. Don't worry. Like 99.999 percent of it is. But the verse numbers and chapter numbers are made up. They're kind gestures from our great-great-great-grandfathers to make the Bible more user friendly. You can imagine how hard it would be if your pastor had to say, "Now everyone flip to halfway through the third sentence of the seventh paragraph of Colossians."

So that big number 4? Moses didn't put it there. He's carrying on with his story about Adam and Eve. When he wants to change the subject or insert a transition, he uses something else, which we'll come across in Genesis 5.

GENESIS 4 // A FRACTURED FAMILY, A FAITHFUL SEED

How does the story of Cain and Abel continue the story of Adam and Eve? By showing us how the first family is fractured by sin. And yet by the time we get to the end of 4:4, we may reasonably wonder what's so different about a sinful world. Eve's loving union with her husband fills the earth with two more image bearers: Cain and Abel. She's fruitful and multiplying. Her sons work hard—Cain tills the soil, Abel shepherds the flock. They're having dominion. They're doing their jobs. Though humanity got off to a rickety start, for a moment it looks like we self-corrected.

Then we read 4:5 and remember that things are not all right.

Why does the Lord reject Cain's offering? It can't be because of the amount; both brought "some." It can't be because God prefers steak over potatoes; later on, he will request vegetarian offerings like Cain's.[1] God's response has little to do with what we find in Cain's hands and everything to do with what he sees in Cain's heart. The Lord knows that Cain is giving his offering faithlessly, regretfully, perhaps with a scowl on his face as he mutters to himself how stupid it is to burn up some of his hard work. Not so with Abel, which is why God looks on him with favor (4:4).[2]

Because Adam failed to crush the serpent in the garden of Eden, sin

---

1. Leviticus 2, for example.
2. Heb. 11:4 confirms this reading, but it's not as though the author of Hebrews gets to his inspired conclusion without evidence. In the Old Testament, whom does the Lord look on with favor? The faithful ones.

now crouches at the door of Cain's heart, greedy for more and more and more. And Cain obliges. His muttering turns to murder.

After Cain kills his brother, the Lord is both severe and merciful. He casts Cain out of his presence and curses Cain to the ground. You could say he now shares the fate of both his biological parents—Adam and Eve—and his spiritual parent—Satan.[3] God is severe toward Cain because sin always carries serious consequences. But he is also merciful. Cain hears about his cursed exile and thinks to himself, "This is a death sentence!" Not so, says the Lord. He yet again treats Cain like his parents when he covers him, not with garments of skin but with a guarantee of safety.

What Moses gives us next (4:17–24) is fascinating. Through a genealogy, he pulls the camera back and tells us more about Cain's family tree. He races through centuries of history to illustrate a sad reality: it's possible to experience God's protection without enjoying his presence. It's possible to carry on a normal and even successful life—to have children and grandchildren, to build cities and contribute to society—and to forget that there's more to life than merely living. Notice the details Moses highlights:

- Cain builds a city and names it after his son, Enoch (4:17).
- Cain's great-great-great-great-great-grandson Lamech marries two women[4] and has three impressive sons: Jabal the agricultural tycoon, Jubal the pop sensation, and Tubal-Cain the international arms dealer (4:19–22).

---

3. In 1 John 3:10–12, Cain's referred to as a child of the devil.

4. Polygamy is unfortunately common for the patriarchs. All of them except Noah and Joseph have multiple wives; many of them sire children through their wives *and* their wives' servants. And yet there's no explicit condemnation of the practice in the book of Genesis or even in the rest of the Torah. Does this mean it's not a problem?

No. As we've already seen, in Gen. 2:24 Moses puts forward the paradigm for marriage. Perhaps it's not surprising that the first person who breaks it is a son of Cain, a seed of the serpent. Throughout the rest of Genesis—and, really, the rest of the Old Testament—polygamy creates terrible problems.

So while God may allow the practice, he certainly doesn't approve of it. Nor does Moses. Which is why he so regularly draws attention to the chaos and sadness it creates.

- Lamech uses the Lord's merciful protection of his family as the basis for his own boastful vengeance (4:23–24).

After surveying more than half a dozen generations, Moses finally stops. Lamech's bloody liturgy makes the point clear: Cain's people might be successful, but they are broken. Sin has knocked and knocked and knocked and they've opened the door over and over and over. They're violent and vindictive, impressive on the outside but dead on the inside. They've taken all the wrong lessons from the Lord's protection, and as a result, they've traded away his presence for their own production.

Sin has fractured the relationship between man and God. That's obvious after Genesis 3. Genesis 4 teaches us that sin has also fractured humanity's first family. Cain's ancestors are materially rich, but spiritually poor. Abel, meanwhile, has no ancestors because his devilish brother killed him. And so the decay of Cain's line poses a problem: how will the Lord make good on his promise to crush sin when the serpent's seeds are reproducing and the women's seeds are all falling to the ground, dead and fruitless?

Moses anticipates that question and so he rewinds the tape to the present.[5] He tells us about another branch of the first family's family tree: "Adam made love to his wife again, and she gave birth to a son and named him Seth, saying, 'God has granted me another child in place of Abel, since Cain killed him.' Seth also had a son, and he named him Enosh" (4:25–26).

For the third time in this chapter, we read about a husband and a wife making love.[6] What will the fruit of their union be this time? More death and decay? Thankfully, no. Moses has some good news for us: "At that time people began to call on the name of the LORD" (4:26).

---

5. Get used to hearing it: Moses is a masterful storyteller.

6. The first (4:1) gives us hope but ends in murder. The second (4:17) starts bad and ends worse. The third (4:25) renews our hope.

GENESIS 5 // MOSES JUMPS
IN A TIME MACHINE

Genealogies are time machines. They fast-forward to the next main character—from Adam to Noah, Noah to Abraham, and so on.[7] We've seen a shortened and simplified one for Cain. The longer ones tend to dwell on the lines of the faithful seeds. In this case, that's Adam's son Seth.

I want to highlight two figures from Seth's family line:

- *Enoch (5:21–24).* Two pieces of Enoch trivia: he's the father of the oldest man who ever lived and he's one of two people who never died.[8] We don't know exactly why the Lord chose to "take him away," but we do know, because Moses tells us twice, that he "walked faithfully with God." Hmm . . . perhaps this cursed pattern of death—notice the repetition of "and then he died" in the verses before this—can be overcome by those who trust in the Lord?

- *Lamech (5:28–31).* We met one Lamech already and he was a bloodthirsty guy. Let's call him Bad Lamech. But this one, Noah's father, is Good Lamech. He sings not about revenge but about redemption: "He will comfort us in the labor and painful toil of our hands caused by the ground the LORD has cursed" (5:29). It's almost as if he's praying that his son will somehow reverse the effects of the curse. Hmm . . . perhaps the cursed effects of sin can be overcome by Noah, the righteous son (6:9) of righteous Lamech.[9]

---

7. For the uninitiated, *fast-forward* is a word borrowed from ye olden times when we watched our movies on VHS tapes. VHS tapes contained movies in a rectangular case that you would put in something called a VCR and then—oh, nevermind, just google it.

8. The second? Elijah (2 Kings 2:11).

9. I am usually dubious of those who find significant meaning behind numbers in Scripture, but it strikes me as a little too convenient that Bad Lamech boasts about his revenge with a math problem: 7 × 77 (4:24). Meanwhile, did you catch how long Good Lamech lives? Which reminds me, why did people live so long? I'll quote the Pharisees in Matt. 21:27: "We don't know." Before the flood, the Lord allowed human life to endure several centuries. After the flood, he does not.

GENESIS 6:1-9:17 // WE END
TO BEGIN AGAIN

So far we've focused on two branches from Adam and Eve's family tree: Cain and Seth. One bad, one good; one cursed like the serpent, one working to bring an end to the cursed serpent. Now, before Moses begins Noah's story, he pulls the camera back yet again to show us a fuller picture of what's going on in the world.

And that picture is not good. Moses describes it in ways that are equal parts supernatural and straightforward. In Genesis 6:2, he tells us, "The sons of God *saw* that the daughters of humans were *beautiful*, and they *married* any of them they chose." Pay attention to the italicized verb-adjective-verb sequence. We've seen it before in Genesis 3:5. Eve *saw* that the fruit was *good* and so she *took* it. In Genesis 6:2, the words are translated differently, but the underlying Hebrew words are identical. Moses frames the behavior of these "sons of God" (saw-attractive-married) the same way he framed the rebellion of Eve (saw-good-took).

That's the straightforward bit. Now on to the supernatural. Who are these "sons of God" that are marrying and multiplying with these "daughters of humans"? Two options exist.

- *Option 1:* They're fallen angels. The strongest case for this is that in the Old Testament, the phrase "sons of God" always refers to angelic beings (Job 1:6; 2:1; 38:7). In this reconstruction, here's what's happening: demons are coming down to earth to have sex with women.
- *Option 2:* The "sons of God" are the godly sons of Seth and they're intermarrying with the wicked daughters of Cain. The strongest case for this is it matches the context and also has the benefit of being less weird.

And yet, despite the weirdness, I'm partial to option 1. Why? Because Moses mentions the Nephilim. Let me explain. With option 2, it's not clear to me why he would bring up the Nephilim at all. With option 1, Genesis 6:1–5's disparate threads seem to come together.

Here's what I mean. Many people say that the Nephilim are the offspring of the "sons of God" and the "daughters of humans," that they're some kind of unholy, inhuman hybrid. But read the text again. Moses never says that, nor does he imply it. Yes, this demon-human union results in "children" (6:4). But these children aren't the Nephilim. They are the "mighty men" (6:4), the kind of heroes an upside-down world celebrates.

Instead, all Moses tells us about the Nephilim is that they "were on the earth in those days—and also afterward." This colorful, contextual detail may confuse us, but it would have comforted his original audience. After all, the Israelites saw the Nephilim *with their own eyes* when they were waiting for them in the promised land (Num. 13:33). And these guys were so big that they made the Israelites feel like grasshoppers.

You can imagine the nervous murmurs. One Israelite tells another, "These guys are so big they can't possibly be human!" Hands shaking, his friend responds, "Maybe they're not." Perhaps rumors were filling the camp that these guys were the demonic demigods they'd heard about from the days of Noah. Moses dispels such spooky speculation with a single detail. His calm historical reflection should calm his friends down. "Friends, the Nephilim were on the earth in those days— and also afterward. They're not who you think they are."

As we begin Genesis 6, clearly, the world is upside down. Do you remember the command God gave to Adam and Eve? "Be fruitful and increase in number; fill the earth with image bearers who reflect my rule." Now look how Moses describes the preflood earth. Human beings are indeed increasing in number (6:1). They're filling the earth— not with righteousness but with violence (6:11). It's as if God steps back and beholds his creation again, and what he sees is not good but corrupt (6:12). Genesis 6:5 offers a bleak but unambiguous summary: "The LORD saw how great the wickedness of the human race had become on the earth, and that every inclination of the thoughts of the human heart was only evil all the time."

The Lord has two responses to this: a pang of regret and a promise to restart.[10] He needs another son, an Adam 2.0. While everything else is upside down, he needs one man who's right side up. This man will be plucked not from the dirt but from the disaster that has become the created order.

In steps Noah, the son of Good Lamech. He's the first person Moses describes as righteous (6:9). It can be tempting to misunderstand *righteous* as strictly moral. So when we hear "Noah was a righteous man," we translate it to something like "Noah was a good guy." He's not violent and wicked like his neighbors. But what made Noah righteous—what made him right side up—was not his relative moral decency but his faith. Like his great-grandfather Enoch, he walked faithfully with God (6:9). Like his great-great-great-great-great-great-grandfather Seth, he found favor in the eyes of the Lord (6:8).

Moses tells us that our new main character is faithful and righteous. And then he shows us what his faith looks like, what righteous people do. They hear the Word of the Lord, they believe it, and then they act.

That's the lesson of Genesis 6:13–7:16. God is verbose with Noah. He gives him lots of instructions in this passage. Make an ark. Cover it with pitch. Here are its dimensions—height, width, depth, the whole nine cubits. Grab a bunch of animals and a bunch of food. Then grab your whole family and get inside this ark, because something called rain will descend on the earth for forty days and forty nights and destroy everything.

Noah, however, is not verbose with the Lord. He obeys without a word. Three times Moses tells us: Noah did everything just as God

---

10. Don't over-read that word *regret*. God isn't up in heaven saying, "Wow! Didn't see this coming. I wish I hadn't done that." Rather, when Moses says God regrets, he's accommodating to our categories of emotion to articulate something true about God's response to rampant wickedness. It displeases him. He does not mean for the world to be like this. Check out 1 Samuel 15, which uses a similar phrase two times. It will clarify this distinction.

commanded him (6:22; 7:5, 16). We can be so easily enamored of and attracted to those who are loud and bold. But some of the best saints are those who quietly obey the Lord.

When Noah hears God's word of judgment, he doesn't snap back like the serpent or snarl like Cain. He believes God has the right to tell him how to live and what to do and so he devotes himself to a task that would take years and would surely elicit the scoffs of his friends and neighbors.

"The Lord said what! Who cares!"

"I'm sorry, did you say 'rain'? What even is rain? You're an idiot!"

Here's the picture Moses paints: The world is lost. But Noah has been found in God's favor because of his faith, a faith that has both made him righteous and determined his path away from destruction and toward deliverance.[11] He does not save himself but relies on the Lord to shut him in (7:16).

There are all sorts of questions we could ask about Noah's floating zoo: Why seven birds? How did Noah know "clean" and "unclean" before Leviticus was even written? Did he take two zebras *and* two thoroughbreds or did he just take two "horse kinds" that, all these centuries later, gave us both zebras and thoroughbreds? We don't need to parse the specifics of the Lord's instructions to understand their substance. Here's the big idea: what goes inside the ark becomes a microcosm of creation because when the rains come, the floating zoo will become a floating paradise. That's why "according to its kind" gets repeated four times in a single verse (7:14). The guts of the ark are another beginning, another Eden that will preserve life. Because once the Lord latches the lock on Noah's ark, death and judgment reign.[12]

Let's pause for a moment and look at Moses' narration of the flood. Pay attention to every word. Try to picture it: "The waters rose and covered the mountains. . . . Every living thing that moved on land perished—birds, livestock, wild animals, all the creatures that swarm

---

11. Heb. 11:7.
12. Forgive the pun.

over the earth, and all mankind. Everything on dry land that had the breath of life in its nostrils died. Every living thing on the face of the earth was wiped out; people and animals and the creatures that move along the ground and the birds were wiped from the earth" (7:20–23).

Imagine it scene by scene. What does this look like? It looks like the de-creation of the world. There are no more animals that move along the ground, creatures of the sixth day. There are no more birds, creatures of the fifth day. Had you ever caught the detail before that all the birds died, too? It's as if the barrage of rain battered them into the sea. Mount Everest—the third day's greatest achievement—has drowned as the waters of judgment erase all distinctions between land and sea.

These descriptions are horrifying. And yet Moses repeats himself. Again and again, he says the same thing: There is nothing left. There is no one left. The world is a graveyard. The world is a graveyard.

A few years ago, I heard a sermon on Noah's ark at a summer camp. After explaining the passage and calling on a few hundred teens to turn from their sin and to trust in Christ, the preacher did something unthinkable. He gave—I don't know what else to call it—a reverse altar call: "If you know for certain that you're not following Christ, I ask you to leave the room and stand outside." Our meeting space was oddly arklike: all wood and high ceilinged, with windows to a large deck. It was nighttime and the lights outside were off. The students who stood up and left didn't disappear to hang out with their friends, they disappeared into darkness. We could see them out there, but barely.[13] We could have heard them, but they made no noise. It was as close to silent as a summer camp can get.

I sat in the back and watched as a few students I knew quite well walked outside. Most didn't surprise me. But a few left me teary-eyed and numb. I saw best friends walk out together. I saw sisters separate, as one took the preacher at his word and left the room. There were

---

13. I called the guy who did this and he said, "I'm not sure I'd do it again."

tears. There were prayers. The preacher took no delight in this illustration. He wasn't intense or impressed with himself. He summed it up simply, with something like, "Those who continue to reject Christ will experience eternal separation and eternal darkness. But there is a place among the people of God where the light is on and the joy is eternal. In Noah's time, that safety came through faith in the Lord, who told him to build an ark. Today it comes through faith in that same Lord, who tells us to trust in his Son, Jesus Christ." I'll never forget that night.[14]

I don't blame kids' books for depicting Noah's ark as a boisterous and buoyant animal party. I don't blame them for rushing toward the rainbow. Because so much of the story is just straight sorrow. A double shot of judgment served neat. But it's true. It's not a metaphor. It's not an illustration. All of it really happened. Moses does not delight in his retelling, and he, too, is neither intense nor impressed. He simply tells the truth. And if we're reading him rightly, we understand that apart from faith in the Lord and favor from the Lord, we're not automatically in the boat with the animals and eight other people. We're under the water. We're outside on the dark deck. We're in the graveyard, where there's no life left.[15]

Finally, when we get to Genesis 8:1, we come up for air: "But God remembered Noah."[16] He has saved his people through judgment, and now it's time to begin again. After the flood's de-creation, it's now the time for re-creation.[17] If we look closely at Genesis 8, we'll notice that Moses depicts these moments in ways that should remind us of Genesis 1. A few similarities:

---

14. I know of at least one person who knew for certain she wasn't following the Lord. That night, for the first time ever, she owned it publicly. More than five years later, she's now a Christian! She points to this night as a significant moment in her walk with the Lord.

15. You might say that so far in Genesis we've learned that the wages of sin is death (Rom. 6:23) and that faith without works is dead (James 2:20).

16. Just like he will remember Abraham in Gen. 19:29 and the people of Israel in Ex. 2:24.

17. I'm confident I first heard this phrase from Sam Emadi. I even once heard him say, "Creation is dying in order to rise again," which is just a bit too crazy to put in the main body, but absolutely good enough for a footnote.

- The Spirit of God hovered over the waters in Genesis 1; in Genesis 8:1, the Spirit reappears as wind[18] over nothing but water. Then the Lord causes the water to recede and the re-creation begins.
- Eventually, the ark comes to rest on land and the distinction between land and sea returns (8:4–5).
- Little by little, the animals return, starting with the birds (8:6–12) and then all the rest (8:15–19). We've already seen that the animals in the ark were arranged "according to their kinds," à la Genesis 1.

The Lord is restarting with Noah and his family what he began with Adam and Eve. Though sin has its roots down deep into the hearts of men, it has not erased their special status or disqualified them from their special job. They're still made in God's image (9:6) and they're still commissioned to be fruitful and fill the earth (9:1, 7).

Of course, not every detail in Genesis 8–9 is identical to Genesis 1–2. For example, the Lord now sanctions Big Macs and pepperoni pizza (9:3). He establishes government, the principle of an eye for an eye (9:5–6). He also promises he will never again flood the earth (9:8–17). He's laid down his bow and placed it in the clouds. But certainly the passages are in conversation with each other.

GENESIS 9:18-28 // WE FALL DOWN AGAIN

By the time we get to Genesis 9:18, Noah and his family are center stage amid a rebuilt creation. So far, Good Lamech has proven to be quite the prophet (5:29). His son Noah has indeed brought relief. But Moses isn't done with Noah yet. There's one more story about his life that Moses wants to tell and, unfortunately, it's a sad one.

It can be understood in at least two ways.

---

18. "Spirit" in 1:2 and "wind" in 8:1 are the same word in Hebrew.

1. THE BAD GUYS' ORIGIN STORY + THE GOOD GUYS' JUSTIFICATION

Let's talk for a bit about Ham. Ham is Noah's son. He is also, Moses tells us twice, "the father of Canaan" (9:18, 22). When we read that description, our minds get a bit fuzzy. Is "Canaan" good or bad? We know that Israel is given Canaan as the promised land, and that's good. So maybe naming your kid Canaan is like naming your kid Eden. It's looking forward to paradise.[19] But we also know that Canaan is filled with, well, Canaanites—and they're bad.[20] So maybe naming your kid Canaan is actually like naming your kid Phil, short for Philistine. Which is it?

The original recipients of this story—Israelites in the wilderness—wouldn't have had the same fuzziness in their minds. They knew the Canaanites as God's enemies, *their* enemies. So when Moses introduces Ham as "the father of Canaan," they'd lurch away in disgust. They'd clinch their fists and click their tongues and long for the day when they would enjoy the land that's rightfully theirs. "May Canaan be the slave of Shem" is a war cry. It's basically saying, "One day, Shem will inherit the promised land."[21]

That history was old hat for Israel. For us? It's probably surprising. But let's back up. How did our hero Noah father the father of the bad guys? Genesis 9:18–28 answers this question with the story that explains the beginning of the Israelite-Canaanite conflict, one that would grow over the course of many generations and intertwine with the histories of many nations.[22]

---

19. For an example of this, consider the hymn "Jerusalem, My Happy Home," which features the verse "Why should I shrink at pain and woe? / Or feel at death dismay? / I've Canaan's goodly land in view, / And realms of endless day."

20. For Canaanites as a reference to Israel's enemies, consider Gen. 15:21. In Genesis 28, when Esau marries a Canaanite, it's clear evidence that he's abandoned the cause of the Lord.

21. The fulfillment of this curse occurs in Josh. 9:27 and 17:12–13 when the sons of Shem conquer some sons of Ham.

22. The Tower of Babel looms as the first detailed episode of this history of Israel versus the World. In fact, Moses alludes to that in 9:19: "These were the three sons of Noah, and from them came the people who were scattered over the whole earth." In other words, they're responsible for the trouble to come.

So that's at least part of what's going on here. This passage offers a clever justification for what's to come both for us as readers—the Table of Nations and the Tower of Babel—and for Israel as the original audience—the conquest of Canaan.

But there's more to understand in this passage.

2. THE FALL 2.0

We already talked about how Genesis 6–8 doubles as a re-creation of the world. Now Moses concludes his flood narrative with a re-creation of the fall. We've begun again, and then we fall down again. We've relived Genesis 1–2; now we must relive Genesis 3.[23]

Consider the shadows of Genesis 3 that creep into this passage:

- Moses describes Noah as a "man of the soil" (9:20) who plants a vineyard. So he's like Adam, working the ground and having dominion over creation (2:15). Yet the only other man of the soil we've met so far is Cain (4:3). So—a mixed bag.
- Like Adam and Eve, Noah takes from the tree and enjoys the actual fruit of his labors. He drinks some wine. But he drinks too much, and so the fruit leads him to sin and his sin leads him to—again, just like Adam and Eve—become naked and ashamed (9:21).
- His two righteous sons act like the Lord when they cover their father's nakedness and shame (9:23). They refuse to join Ham in his unrighteous, flippant mockery.[24]
- After Ham's sin, it's as though Noah stands in the place of God when he utters curses against Canaan (9:24).

---

23. *Ahem* Moses is a masterful storyteller.

24. We don't have all the details about the situation here. For example, we don't know how Noah found out what Ham had done. But we can infer enough from the details we do have that Ham's behavior was unambiguously unrighteous. At the very minimum, he dishonored his father by responding flippantly to his dire circumstances.

• After Noah's sin, the curse of sin finally comes for him, too. Noah was a righteous and blameless man, the best of his era. But he was not a perfect man.

Look back to that genealogy in Genesis 5. How does every entry end?[25] He died and he died and he died and he died.

Once upon a time, Good Lamech looked at the face of his son and saw a spark of hope, of relief. But by the end of Genesis 9, we realize that whatever fulfillment Noah ushered in is only temporary. Any spark of lasting hope has been extinguished—not as quickly as Abel's life but just as decisively.

"After the flood Noah lived 350 years. Noah lived a total of 950 years, and then he died" (9:28–29).

He died and he died and he died.

So we get to the end of Genesis 9 and we're suddenly adrift in a rebuilt world that's still stained by sinful men. Where's the relief? Where's the comfort? And how do we make it last for good?

---

25. Again, except Enoch, which suggests the pattern of death is not entirely irreversible.

FOUR

GENESIS 10–11

What's your name?

Slap!

It doesn't matter what your name is.

–THE ROCK

Knock-knock-knockin' on heaven's door.

–GUNS N' ROSES, "KNOCKIN' ON HEAVEN'S DOOR"

We've already seen that genealogies in Genesis are time machines. They fast-forward from one main character to the next—Adam to Noah, Noah to Abraham, and so on. But the genealogy ahead tweaks that template. Instead of fast-forwarding, Genesis 10 is primarily concerned with foreshadowing.

What happened to these sons of Noah that will require the intervention of the Lord through Abraham? We're about to find out.

GENESIS 10 // BREADCRUMBS TOWARD BABEL

Moses has already told us the most relevant information about Ham, Shem, and Japheth: "From them came the people who were scattered over the whole earth." When he mentions that in Genesis 9:19, he's craning his neck and looking toward the future. So before Moses tells us *that* story, he gives us some details about who these guys are.

He begins with the sons of Japheth. They're sea people who spread out according to language and clan (10:1–5). Do you recognize any of them? Maybe one or two. There's Magog, whom you may be familiar with if you're really into apocalyptic literature.[1] There's also Gomer, whom you may be familiar with if you've spent some time in Hosea.[2] But these overlaps are incidental. They don't tell us much, if anything.

Let's skip Ham for a second and move on to the sons of Shem, Noah's favored son (10:21–31). He receives pride of place in Noah's only recorded words (9:25–27). Why? Because he honored his father by refusing to look on his nakedness. As a result, Shem becomes the blessed father of the Hebrew people.[3] Unlike their maritime cousins, the Semites spread throughout the hill country. Do you recognize any of these folks? To be honest, I didn't the first time I read Genesis 10, and I still don't. We get a curious detail about a guy named Peleg— during his time, the earth was "divided"—and that's about it. (I assume that's just saying he was around during the Tower of Babel.)

Now let's spend some time with Ham's kids (10:6–20). We already know his bloodline is cursed (9:25). We also know he's the father of—cue the ominous music—Canaan and therefore his brood of Canaanites. Moses has told us this more than once. As we start to really dig into his family tree, we run across some familiar faces. So if Ham's unsavory offspring is familiar even to us, thousands of years later, you can imagine how the Israelites would have received this information. By retracing Ham's history, Moses is giving us the origin story for Israel's enemies—past, present, and future.

Let's list some of the usual suspects, starting with the most notorious:

---

1. Ezek. 38:2; 39:6; Rev. 20:8.

2. Or Mayberry.

3. If you've ever wondered about the etymology of the word *anti-Semitism*, it comes from Genesis 10. Anti-Semitism is anti-Shem. Also, we get the word *Hebrew* from Eber, who shows up in 10:21, 24, and 25.

- *Egypt (10:6).* Voldemort is to Harry Potter as Egypt is to Israel. To borrow a line from Martin Luther, Egypt is their "ancient foe." The Israelites had just spent four hundred years under the thumb of this particular son of Ham. Though there would be a season when the relationship would be bloodless and benign,[4] in the more recent decades under Moses the Egyptians reveled in their ruthlessness to God's people.
- *Kasluhites (Philistines; 10:13).* In the Torah, the Philistines aren't yet public enemy number 1. But they will be. Just wait.
- *Nimrod (10:8–12).* Did you know this playground insult was inspired by a real guy? He may not be familiar to you, but I bet the kingdoms he built are: Babylon (10:10) and Assyria (10:11). And guess what two kingdoms, several centuries later, would conquer Israel before casting them into exile? Babylon and Assyria. It's striking to me that Moses describes Nimrod as "a mighty hunter." Like Jabal the agricultural tycoon, Jubal the pop sensation, and Tubal-Cain the international arms dealer from Genesis 4:19–22, Moses focuses on outwardly impressive descriptions for inwardly broken men. More on Nimrod in a second.
- *The Ignominious, Amalgamated "Ites" (10:13–19).* Jebusites, Amorites, Girgashites, and on and on and on. These various Canaanite clans show up a lot throughout the Old Testament—not always all together, rarely in the same packaging, but in every case, they're presented as a kind of amalgamated shorthand for "enemies of God."[5]

Again, here's the big idea: Genesis 10 provides context for the concluding scene of Genesis' opening act (Genesis 11). Genesis 10 describes a world spread out from the eastern hills to the western seas. It tells the backstory of all the nations of the earth, focusing its

---

4. See Genesis 37–50.

5. For an incomplete list of passages that include threats from the "Ites": Ex. 3:8, 17; 13:5; 23:23; 33:2; 34:11; Num. 13:29; Deut. 7:1; 20:17. That's just in the Torah! Other times, like in Gen. 28:1, Moses just uses *Canaanite* as a synecdoche to refer to all enemies of God.

attention on "the bad guys" or, to use Genesis 3's language, "seeds of the serpent."

A lot has changed since Genesis 1. The one blessed family—bone of bone, flesh of flesh—has multiplied into diverse clans, and these diverse clans have dispersed throughout the known world. They don't live together, they don't worship together, and they don't even, it turns out, speak the same language (10:4, 20, 31). They're strangers in the same land.

How did we get here? In Genesis 11, Moses rewinds the tape to show us.

GENESIS 11:1-9 // A REWIND TO NIMROD'S NIMRODDERY

Are you familiar with the word *aptronym*? It's just a fancy way of saying "an apt name," of noticing that someone's name just so happens to describe them. Obvious examples show up all the time in fiction. For example, there's *The Pilgrim's Progress*, in which characters have names like Obstinate and Mr. Great-heart and Child-of-Divorce-So-That's-Where-the-Self-Deprecating-Sense-of-Humor-Comes-From.[6] Less obvious examples include Daddy Warbucks from *Annie*, who, if you can believe it, made his bucks off the war. The phenomenon some-times shows up in real life, too. William Wordsworth wrote worthy words. Chris Moneymaker shocked the world by making money, win-ning the 2003 main event of the World Series of Poker as an amateur. Usain Bolt is as fast as lightning. You get the point.

In Genesis 11, we get the story of one of my favorite aptronyms: Nimrod. You're probably like, "Um, Alex, *you're* a nimrod—that name doesn't even show up in this chapter!" You're right. But the Tower of Babel is proof that Nimrod is, well, a nimrod. It's a flashback that

---

6. I'm doing this from memory, so perhaps those examples aren't *exactly* right.

explains how that grandson of Ham, that "mighty hunter before the LORD," tried to drag humanity up into the throne room of heaven and, in the process, ended up dispersing humanity to the corners of the earth.

How do we know it's a flashback? Moses doesn't insert a scrolling aside that says "a long time ago in a neighborhood across the street." No, we know it's a flashback because of what Moses says about language and because of its location.

- *Language.* Look at 11:1. How many languages are there in the world? One. But Moses told us three times in the previous chapter (10:4–5, 20, 31) that these scattered nations no longer spoke the same language.
- *Location.* Look at 11:2. What's the setting for what we're about to read? Shinar. That's where the Tower of Babel was built. Now look back to 10:10 and pay attention to the places Moses connects to Nimrod: "The first centers of [Nimrod's] kingdom were Babylon, Uruk, Akkad and Kalneh, in Shinar." Of course, the chronology isn't spelled out precisely here. So it's possible these tower-building plans happened only after Nimrod died. But Moses clearly connects Babel not only to the offspring of Ham in general but to the oversight of Nimrod in particular.

So when we slow down and pay attention to the details, we realize that the setup of the story helps us understand its emphasis. Though Moses doesn't name any names, the antagonists of Genesis 11:1–9 aren't anonymous. The rebellion isn't perpetrated by nameless, faceless nobodies. It's premeditated by the cursed sons of Noah, seeds of the serpent, and the project manager was likely a nimrod named Nimrod.[7]

That's the who. Now let's focus for a second on the what and the

---

7. A bit more on Nimrod: his name likely means "rebel," and he becomes in a very real sense the prototypical rebel not only in Genesis but throughout the rest of Scripture. He builds Babel, which becomes Babylon, which is the antithesis to God's kingdom all the way until Revelation. (Check out Revelation 17–19.)

why. What did these people want to do, why did they want to do it, and why was it so wrong, so stupid, so nimrodish? Notice that they didn't just want to build a tower in the middle of an empty field: "Come, let us build ourselves *a city*, with a tower that reaches to the heavens" (11:4). The tower isn't meant to be an accent or an accoutrement but the socioreligious centerpiece of an entire man-centered world.

It's quite obvious why this is both sinful and stupid. First of all, it's impossible! You can't pierce the heavens with technological ingenuity and humanitarian cooperation.

But there's another problem, too, that's tethered more closely to our story so far. Did you notice that the Babel builders gave two reasons for their behavior? There's a divine one and an earthly one. We discussed the former already. Now here's the rest of the verse: "otherwise we will be scattered over the face of the whole earth" (11:4).

Building the Tower of Babel was both a sinful rebellion *and* a sinful retreat. It was a rebellion against our Creator because it was a retreat from his commands. After all, the Lord had been clear: "Be fruitful, fill the earth, and reflect my righteous rule to the watching world." What a joyous job! Now these sons of Ham have been clear with the Lord: "We don't want to spread out and worship *you*. We want to stay put and worship ourselves."

Like Adam and Eve, they've rejected God's word and God's rule. Like Cain's sons, they're building cities and naming them after themselves. And now their plan is about to be thwarted.

I love how Moses records God's response: it's sarcastic, even biting. It's as if he's squinting from above, and Moses tells us he has to "come down" to see this tower that was supposed to knock-knock-knock on heaven's door.[8] Then he mocks their clumsy initiative with an identical refrain: "Come, let's go down and wreck their plan" (compare 11:3 with 11:7). And then he does exactly that.

---

8. Did you know that the Guns N' Roses' well-known hair-metal ballad was a cover of a 1973 Bob Dylan song?

Their plans fail at every turn. By the end of the story, they're not storming the throne room of heaven, because they're scattered throughout the world. They can no longer "make a name" for themselves because they now go by many different names. Their once united cause is now lost.

It's worth pausing for a moment to talk about how easy it is to waste our lives pursuing horizontal, humanitarian accomplishments. Here's what I mean. Building the Tower of Babel wasn't just one guy's harebrained idea. The plan seems to have captured the imagination of everybody. You might even say that Genesis 11 depicts men and women using the best of their technology—bricks and mortar—in the pursuit of an urgent social cause—"We must make a name for ourselves!"

If you're near your phone, open up Instagram or Facebook or YouTube. If you're reading this on a city bus, look outside. If you're listening to this in your car, keep your eyes on the road. What do we see everywhere we look? Urgent invitations to activism. Exciting opportunities for making our lives count. Curated ads to buy stuff that will make the world a better, more enjoyable place. Things are hardly different today than they were thousands of years ago. The temptations remain the same even as the technologies evolve. Give your life to this or that cause: end racism, protect reproductive justice, expose election fraud, get water to people who will die without it, defund the police, protect our borders. I could keep going, but you get the point. Our world's various mission statements dovetail with Nimrod's life goal: work with your fellow humans to make this world a better place for future humans.

But the message of the Bible is simple: the height of human achievement can't access the heavens. We were made for more, and anything we pursue without reference to God is ultimately a waste of time or, still worse, the waste of a life.[9]

---

9. This doesn't mean you have to be a monk or a pastor or a nun. Doing something "in reference to God" means obeying Col. 3:23–24. Look it up. And let those verses shape the way

A few years ago, I ate lunch with a friend at the base of the Burj Khalifa. At more than 150 stories, the Burj is the tallest building in the world. It is the actual height of human achievement.

Now, I'm a sucker for a good spectacle. That's why I still kind of like professional wrestling. So I kept asking my friend question after question. Have you been to the top? Does it sway? Were you scared? What goes on in all those rooms? How far does it go *under*ground?

Here's what I learned: there are tons of empty floors. He told me, "People say Russian dudes buy floors and keep them empty to launder money. It's safer to have your cash tied up in real estate and not . . . other things." He gave me a look. I gave him the same look. *Ah, I see.* This conversation made it clear to me: the closer you get to the wonders of this world, the less impressive they get.

I basically already knew that. But then he told me something new: the Burj's first hundred floors are a mixture of hotel rooms, extravagant apartments, and office space. The top fifty floors? All office space. "Why?" I asked. "Wouldn't fancy rich people want to live up at the top so that they could literally look down on the world?"

"Yeah, some people wanted to," he said. "But the engineers eventually realized that people couldn't sleep there. Human bodies can't be horizontal that high for eight hours without messing up their equilibrium."

Hmm, maybe the Lord's trying to tell us something.

GENESIS 11:10-32 // A FAST-FORWARD TO ABRAM'S OBEDIENCE

By tracing the lineage from Shem to Abram, Moses ends his prologue of Genesis. He rewound the tape at the beginning of Genesis 11 to show

---

you watch movies and post Instagram stories and grill veggies and play twenty-five straight games of Bananagrams with your granddaughter who can't even read.

us the story of the Tower of Babel because it's the perfect contrast with what's to come. The rebellious nations set up the redeemed nation. Moses then concludes Genesis 11 with a traditional genealogy that fast-forwards and introduces us to the next slew of main characters. We're done with Noah and Shem and, nearly a thousand years later, we're on to Abram and Lot. Abram settles in with his nephew, who is basically his son. Moses tells us that Abram and Sarai couldn't have kids because she "was not able to conceive" (11:30).

So that's all we know about Abram so far: he's married to a barren woman and he's settled in a new home.[10]

GENESIS 1-11 // A RETROSPECTIVE

What's happened so far in our story?

Humankind has been created and cursed. The Lord has promised to do something about this, but not yet. Instead, brother has turned against brother, and humanity has turned in on itself, filling the earth with violence and evil. Creation has been destroyed and rebuilt. More recently, the sons of our hero Noah have raised their fists toward the Lord and craned their necks toward heaven. The Lord sees, he laughs, and now humanity is far flung and dispersed to the four corners of the earth.

The rest of Genesis—and, really, the rest of the Old Testament[11]— tells the story of how God begins to make good on his promise in Genesis 3:15, how he uses one family and then one nation to undo the curses of death and sin and separation from God. Genesis is the family story. Exodus through the end of the Old Testament is the nation story.

Genesis tells the story of how the family that gave birth to this nation is beautifully, invitingly unique and yet—sometimes in the same breath—boringly, unsurprisingly common. It tells the story of God's

---

10. Josh. 24:2 adds that Abram's family "worshiped other gods," which we can perhaps intuit given their Babel-adjacent homes of Ur and the newly named Haran.

11. And, really-really, the rest of the whole Bible!

presence and God's absence, of God's salvation and God's judgment, of promises made and promises refused and promises made yet again, of evil turned to good and death turned to life. Moses is a masterful storyteller.

That family, of course, is Abram's family. That nation, of course, is Israel. She begins like every nation before her: with the birth of a man who will become her father. And she will persist as every nation before her: with the birth of one son and another son and more sons after that. And yet Israel is not like other nations. She is peculiar because she's founded on promises uttered from the throne room of heaven, promises that include—especially after the events we've just seen—a rather shocking assertion: "I will make your name great."

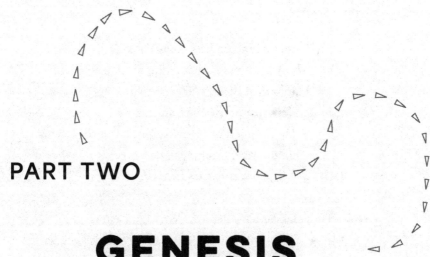

PART TWO

GENESIS
12:1–25:18

Father Abraham had many sons.
Many sons had Father Abraham.
I am one of them, and so are you.
So let's just praise the Lord.
Right arm, left arm, right foot, left foot,
Chin up, turn around, sit down.

–AUTHOR UNKNOWN

Phil: "Do you ever have déjà vu, Mrs. Lancaster?"

Mrs. Lancaster: "I don't think so, but I could check with the kitchen."

–GROUNDHOG DAY

FIVE

GENESIS 12-14

All that glisters is not gold—
Often have you heard that told.
Many a man his life hath sold
But my outside to behold.
Gilded tombs do worms enfold.
Had you been as wise as bold,
Young in limbs, in judgment old,
Your answer had not been inscrolled.
Fare you well. Your suit is cold.

—WILLIAM SHAKESPEARE, *THE MERCHANT
OF VENICE*, ACT II, SCENE 7

Sometimes a man wants to be stupid if it lets
him do a thing his cleverness forbids.

—JOHN STEINBECK, *EAST OF EDEN*

At the end of Genesis 11, humankind is scattered without a solution. At the beginning of Genesis 12, that begins to change. The promises God makes to Abram are essential to understanding the rest of Genesis. So let's slow down and make sure we understand them.

GENESIS 12:1 // THE LORD'S AUDACIOUS COMMAND

It's easy to imagine Abram and Sarai settled down and childless in Haran, wasting away their days. They have no progeny and no prospects. Then the Lord shows up and gives Abram a job to do: go.

Trust me, he says. Leave the comfort and security you enjoy and follow me. He's not offering to connect Abram to a Mesopotamian realtor so that he and his family can get in now while interest rates and costs of living are low. He's commanding him to leave their support structures and protection in Haran and go somewhere the Lord will eventually show him.

GENESIS 12:2-5 // ABRAM'S WALK DOWN THE AISLE

Perhaps the Lord anticipates resistance to this audacious request, so he reassures Abram with three promises:

- *"I will make you into a great nation."* We can't forget the immediate context. In Genesis 11, Moses gave us the origin story of *all* nations. Now it's as if the Lord leans back, cracks his knuckles, and says, "Now I'm going to make a nation of my own." What are his ingredients? Not verdant gardens guarded by strategic hills. Not mighty hunters or coastal elites. He's going to use anonymous land and fill it with a nondescript nomad and his barren wife.
- *"I will make your name great."* Again, we can't forget the context. After the Tower of Babel—that dumb debacle that led to the division of humankind—God promises to do for one man what all of humankind could not accomplish for itself. Hopefully we get the lesson by now. From Cain to Lamech to Nimrod's

subcontractors, we can't make a name for ourselves, and when we try, things go really bad really fast. The Lord's surprising kindness is on full display here as he promises to give as a gift what we tried and failed to earn for ourselves.[1]

- *"I will bless you. . . . You will be a blessing. . . . I will bless those who bless you, and whoever curses you I will curse."* The Lord promises to make Abram a blessing. How? First, by blessing Abram himself. Second, by blessing those who bless Abram and cursing those who curse him. So far in Genesis, who's been cursed? Those who have rejected the Lord. So when he promises to bless those who bless Abram and curse those who don't, he's basically saying, "How people respond to you will be how they respond to me."

You could summarize Genesis 12:1–3 as follows: The Lord will give Abram unknown land. He will provide for Abram offspring that will one day graduate from family and clan to nation. Some of those offspring will even be kings. But there's more. These promises to Abram aren't private and provincial. The Lord's not promoting Abram to village chieftain. No, the creator of the heavens and the earth is placing a nondescript nomad and his barren wife at the center of his promises to reverse the curse and bless the world: "All peoples on earth will be blessed *through you.*"

I've argued that Genesis 3:15–20 functions as a kind of skeleton key for unlocking the emphases of the Old Testament. So we should pay attention to how this passage is in conversation with that one. After man's first sin, the Lord curses the land with thorns, the reproductive process with pain, and the family structure with rivalry.[2] Land, seed, human relationships—all cursed after Adam and Eve's sin.

---

1. It's appropriate to see hints of royalty in this promise, too. Those will become clearer as we keep reading Genesis (17:6, "kings will come from you"). Later on in the Old Testament, in 2 Sam. 7:9, the Lord reiterates the Abrahamic promises to King David ("I will make your name great").

2. It's not as though the Lord curses only husbands and wives, because in the very next

Do you see how these promises to Abram spark the reversal of all that? Land, seed, human relationships—all offered as gifts and blessings. The Lord promises land as a gift. He promises abundant offspring as a gift—so abundant that a family will become a clan and a clan will become a nation. He promises to halt the enmity of man against woman—of brother against brother, country against country— through whatever he has in store for Abram. The Lord will bless the world and overcome the curse of sin through the seed of Abram.[3]

The fog is beginning to fade. The seed of the woman who will one day crush the head of the serpent is also the seed of Seth and Shem and now Abram and Sarai, that nondescript nomad and his barren wife. I keep repeating that phrase because the recipients of these promises are almost as shocking as their details. Clearly, this plan to bless world will happen only through God's power and wisdom, not man's.

The primary goal of this book is to give you a guided tour of Genesis. I hope you like what you see. The Bible is amazing, isn't it? But I would be a terrible tour guide if I failed to steal us away from Moses for a second so that we can look at how one New Testament passage summarizes the events of Genesis 12.

When the apostle Paul read Genesis 12:1–3, here's what he saw: "Scripture foresaw that God would justify the Gentiles by faith, and announced the gospel in advance to Abraham: 'All nations will be blessed through you'" (Gal. 3:8).[4] If Genesis 3:15 is Scripture's first gospel-centered sentence, then Genesis 12:3 is its second. Did Abram know this seed's name would be Jesus? No. Did he know this seed would be both human and divine? Probably not. Did he know this seed

---

chapter, we have brother murdering brother. The rot of the cursed family starts at the top and goes down to the roots.

3. Jim Hamilton taught me this during episode 4 of *Bible Talk*. This promise is so important that it shows up again and again throughout Scripture. Here are my receipts: Gen. 22:18; 26:4; 28:14; Ex. 33:1; 2 Samuel 7; Psalm 72; Jer. 4:2; Acts 3:25; Gal. 3:8. Like a family heirloom, this blessing gets passed along until it is fulfilled and even expanded in Jesus.

4. We'll return to this passage again when we talk about Genesis 22, but for now we can just focus on a few verses.

would die a cursed death on the cross to cancel the curse for his future offspring? Almost certainly not.

And yet despite Abram's inability to outfox the Lord's surprising sovereignty, he did know how to respond to such extravagant, incredible promises—with faith. Moses records his faith with little fanfare: "So Abram went, as the LORD had told him" (12:4). This faith would soon falter and fail, but it wasn't fake. He lifted up his life and took everything he had because he trusted the Lord.

The apostle Paul isn't making stuff up. He's not misreading or overspiritualizing Moses. He sees in the life of Israel's patriarch a pattern that must characterize every Christian. He sees that Genesis 12's fulfillment is Jesus Christ, and the appropriate response—the only means to access the Lord's promised blessing—is faith in Jesus Christ. That's why he can follow up Galatians 3:8 with another jaw-dropping verse: "So those who rely on faith are blessed *along with Abraham*, the man of faith" (Gal. 3:9).

The promises of Genesis 12 may seem distant and irrelevant. They are, after all, thousands of years old and given to a man from a country you've never been to. But these promises to bless are still held out to all who believe in Jesus, and these threats to curse still hang over all who refuse him. Remember, he's already told Abram, "How people respond to you will be how they respond to me."

Genesis is far from defunct. Its urgency should both thrill and startle us.

GENESIS 12:6-20 // THE UNFULFILLMENT

The Lord doesn't leave Abram in the dark long as to what land he's promised him. It's Canaanite land and—no surprise—it's full of Canaanites. He responds by building an altar and worshiping the Lord. Altars show up a lot in the Old Testament and, generally speaking, you should associate them with worship.

Eventually, a famine comes (12:10), so Abram relocates to Egypt. You might be tempted to think, *Egypt, why Egypt! They're the bad guys.* But I wouldn't be too hard on Abram for avoiding starvation. The problem isn't necessarily going to Egypt but what he does once he gets there.

Our heroes have let us down before. Adam ate the fruit, Noah drank the fruit, and now Abram sells out his wife as a sex slave. When Moses writes, after remarking on Sarai's beauty, "she was taken into his palace," he's being polite. When he writes "[Pharaoh] treated Abram well for her sake," he's not being polite. He's sticking his finger in Abram's chest and saying, "You idiot! Don't you realize what you're doing!"

In case you vicariously feel Moses' finger somewhere near your own sternum, let me explain why he's so mad. First of all, he's mad because Abram's an awful husband. Notice his fear: these Egyptians are going to think Sarai is so pretty that they'll—oh, no!—kill him and let her live (12:12). So he hatches a plan to protect not his wife but himself, which also happens to enrich himself (12:13). Abram puts Sarai in lots of danger to avoid any danger for himself. This is wicked behavior. Good husbands die for their wives (Eph. 5:25–30), they don't sell them out.

But there's more to say. Abram's behavior here not only jeopardizes the Lord's promises to him, it results in their temporary reversal. Let me explain.

The former is certainly more obvious than the latter. Abram has just been promised that he will bear offspring that will eventually become a nation that will eventually bless every other nation. For this to happen, he needs to have a son—and to have a son, he needs his wife not to be "in the palace" of another man, much less a man who is the king of a pagan nation. His selfishness jeopardizes the Lord's promises to him.

But the problem runs deeper than this. Remember, the Lord promised that all the nations of the world would be blessed through Abram, provided that they join him in his chorus of faith. Did you notice how Abram's plan unfolds? Well, it works! Moses tells us: "[Pharoah] treated

Abram well for her sake, and Abram acquired sheep and cattle, male and female donkeys, male and female servants, and camels" (12:16). But this is all backward. Here's why: in Genesis 12:10–16, Abram is blessed by the nations with temporary blessings because of his unbelief. But the point of this whole thing was for Abram to bless the nations himself with eternal blessings because they've followed his genuine belief. The events in Egypt are a temporary reversal of the Lord's promised paradigm. They're *unfulfillments*, if that's even a word.

Sometimes, when we're stuck in sin, we realize it and wake up. Other times, God plagues kings of pagan nations so that we're forced to see how stupid we are. That's what happens here in Egypt. The Lord intervenes and rescues Sarai from the degradation of Pharaoh's bed and the selfishness of her husband. Abram is no hero here. He's not a conduit of blessing to the nations. Far from it, he's a conduit for cursing. At the end of Genesis 12, Abram silently slinks home, richer in stuff but poorer in what really matters (13:2). And he probably has to sleep on the couch.[5]

GENESIS 13 // CE N'EST PAS . . .

Our family recently visited Washington, DC. We filled our days with the usual touristy, kid-friendly stuff. We rode scooters on the National Mall, and watched our kids cry after crashing their scooters into each other on the National Mall. We cried out of fear of the Metro, and we

---

5. My friend Sam Emadi loves the exodus. He sees it everywhere, like in Gen. 12:10–20. He says that this episode "prefigures the exodus." That's a fancy way of saying that Moses realized the Lord had sovereignly planned certain events of Abram's life such that they corresponded with Israel's future. And that's a fancy way of saying Abram experiences first what Israel experiences later.

If you're curious, here are the relevant connections: both stories feature a famine in the land that forces Israel into Egypt, at which point someone is sold into slavery only to be rescued once the Lord brings a plague on Pharaoh's house. Oh, and in both stories, Pharaoh allows them to leave with a bunch of their stuff! According to Sam, Moses knows his audience and so he draws attention to these correspondences so that they will see this "paradigm for deliverance." The Lord saved Israel's mother in the same way he saved Israel.

For more on this, see *Bible Talk*, episode 4.

cried out of sadness because we didn't want to get off the Metro. My favorite memory? When my son Johnny kept setting off laser-triggered alarms at the National Portrait Gallery because he cozied up to that famous Gilbert Stuart painting of George Washington. A disembodied voice communicated its displeasure: "You are too close to the exhibit. Please step back." Through his painted pursed lips, our first president did, too. I laughed. My wife did not.

Later that afternoon, we walked to the White House. It was a hot, humid, hot-dog-from-a-street-cart kind of day. As we neared 1600 Pennsylvania Avenue, I noticed a family feverishly taking photos. The dad, who looked like Salvador Dali with a beret, asked me in French to take a photo. His spastic gestures made it clear that I had to get the building behind them in the frame.

As I took his iPhone, I peeked behind them and saw a large and beautiful white building. Its facade was marked by formidable white columns. Above those white columns were these words: "THE DEPARTMENT OF TREASURY."

I could have said, "Ce n'est pas la maison blanche."[6] Perhaps I should have. But I didn't have the heart. So I smiled and snapped the photo.

Sometimes, like French tourists, we think we're looking at one thing but we're really looking at something else. Maybe we have the wrong information, the wrong intuition, or the wrong source of authority. Maybe we're getting jobbed by a jerk who should just tell us the truth.

Genesis 13 is a story about mixed-up people and their mixed-up perception. We've already seen this about Abram. He's mixed-up. He's faithful and fearful. He's a bundle of initiative and iniquity. He believes and he misbehaves. And yet over these next two chapters, we get two stories that chart Abram's progress and culminate in the Lord's assertion of his righteousness (15:6).

After Abram and Lot return home, Abram seems repentant: "There

---

6. Translation: "This is not the White House." Okay, so yeah, I took a few years of French. I probably could have mangled my way toward the devastating truth. But it was hot—and humid.

Abram called on the name of the LORD" (13:4). But there's a problem. Bethel ain't big enough for the both of them, so they need to separate. Like a good uncle, he lets Lot decide his lot (13:8–9). The last time Abram came up with a solution, it was self-serving and sinful. Here, he gets it right.

Lot, meanwhile, does not. I wonder if you noticed Moses' clues that Lot has made a terrible decision:

Clue 1: Moses' Curious Description. "Lot looked around and saw that the whole plain of the Jordan toward Zoar was well watered, like the garden of the LORD, like the land of Egypt" (13:10).

When Moses describes Lot's chosen land as both Edenic and Egyptian, he's lifting the curtain on Lot's halfhearted, mixed-up worldview. He's attracted to its shortsighted benefits—water! protection! prosperity!—and ambivalent about eternal ones. Who cares that this place looks like Egypt? The prosperity he and his uncle received there came at a significant price. And who cares that it looks like Eden? The garden wasn't paradise because of its shaded pools and verdant pastures. It was paradise because the Lord was there—and he's long since locked the gates and asked his flaming-sword-wielding angels to stand at the ready.

Lot wants the appearance of paradise with the Lord *and* the prosperity of this world. But he can't have both. It's a mirage. It's glittering fool's gold. Lot thinks he's smiling with his family in front of the president's home, but in reality, the only thing behind him is a bunch of pencil pushers grinding their way toward a mediocre retirement. That will soon become clear.[7]

Clue 2: Lot's Ominous Direction. "So Lot . . . set out toward the east" (13:11). John Steinbeck didn't pick the title *East of Eden* because he adored alliteration. He chose it because "east of Eden" means "away

---

7. Moses also wants us to see similarities between Lot and Eve. In Genesis 3, Eve "saw that the tree was good for food, and that it was a delight to the eyes" and so she "took of its fruit and ate" (3:6 ESV). In Genesis 13, Lot "lifted up his eyes and *saw* that the Jordan Valley was" good for a home, "so Lot chose [took] for himself all the Jordan Valley" (13:10–11 ESV). The ESV more clearly connects the two passages by highlighting the movement of their eyes.

from God's presence." Or more simply, "east of Eden" means "uh-oh." In Genesis 4:16, Cain flees east to wander toward Nod. In Genesis 11:2, Nimrod's crew moves east until they settle down in Shinar, where they build that stupid tower. So when we discover that Lot chose land to the east, we should think to ourselves, *Uh-oh.*

Clue 3: Lot's New Neighbors. "Lot settled among the cities of the valley and moved his tent as far as Sodom. Now the men of Sodom were wicked, great sinners against the LORD" (13:12–13 ESV). If you're familiar at all with what comes next, you'll know that this bit of foreshadowing is the *coup de grâce.*[8] Lot has faced a fork in the road, and rather than taking the right path, he has stepped on that fork and it's hit him square in the face. He's in trouble now.

Moses then gives us the details about Abram's resettlement. The differences are telling. Remember, we're charting Abram's progress. After Lot "lifted up his eyes" (ESV translation of 13:10) now the Lord commands Abram to "lift up" his eyes (ESV, 13:14). God then re-ups and one-ups his promises to Abram: "*All* this land will be yours, and it will be filled by so many of your kids that no one will even be able to count them. Now go and enjoy it" (my translated summary of 13:15–17). While Lot is salivating over his land's agricultural promise, the Lord is reminding Abram to trust in his promises above anything else.[9]

Moses ends this episode by describing Abram's faithful obedience just like he did the last time: "So Abram went" (13:18; cf. 12:4). The point of Genesis 13 is quite clear: though the prospects of the world can be enticing to the eyes, they're never better than the promises of the Lord. The world is full of fake Edens that resemble paradise but in reality lead us toward hell. Lot didn't realize this. He thought he was walking toward a wellspring of water, but actually he was walking toward destruction.[10]

---

8. In fact, the foreshadowing started with that parenthetical in 13:10 that explains that Lot's land looked so enticing only because the Lord had not yet turned it—and his wife—into a heap of salt.

9. For more on this passage, consider Iain Duguid's response to a forum question about Gen. 13:10 here: www.puritanboard.com/threads/question-in-genesis-13-10.111419/.

10. Some of us need to hear this warning—like right now.

Lot lifted up his eyes and riveted them to the luscious and lucrative land. He lived by sight. So he hurled himself east. Abram lifted up his eyes and riveted them to the promises of the Lord. He believed the Lord would make good on his promises to give him land and children to fill that land. He lived by faith even as the circumstances of his life cried foul, because he knew that wherever the Lord is, there is protection and prosperity. There is paradise.

GENESIS 14:1-16 // NOT YOUR AVERAGE OCTOGENARIAN

Growing up, when I thought of Abram and Sarai, I imagined two old people waiting in some kind of yurtlike home until the Lord magically gave them a baby. Perhaps they passed the time by playing stone dominoes or doing, via cuneiform, the *Canaan Daily Times* crossword puzzle. I obviously didn't read my Bible very much.

Abram and Sarai aren't two octogenarian retirees. They've got more money and livestock than they know what to do with (13:2). They've got hardworking herders in their employ (13:7). By the time we get to Genesis 14, Moses tells us that Abram has 318 trained men who were *born in his household*. This is no ramshackle militia. This is the Abrahamic Task Force, the true and better ATF.

But I've gotten ahead of myself.

Genesis 14 tells a story about a war between kings that eventually provokes a response from Abram. But first, Moses sets the stage. This war has two teams—for simplicity, we'll call them the Mesopotamia Monarchs and the Promised-Land Promised Ones. Here are their starting lineups:[11]

---

11. Cue the music the Jordan-era Bulls used during warmups, which I just learned is called "Sirius" and was made by the British rock band called the Alan Parsons Project.

The Mesopotamia Monarchs

- *Amraphel.* He's the king of Shinar, which is where Nimrod's people came from.
- *Arioch.* He's the king of Ellasar. We don't really know anything about him except that Ellasar means "tall." So he probably played center.
- *Kedorlaomer.* He's their Michael Jordan, the boss. More on him in a second.
- *Tidal.* He's the king of Goyim, which means "nation." So he's the king of a nation called Nation. How cool.

The Promised-Land Promised Ones

- *Bera.* King of Sodom.
- *Birsha.* King of Gomorrah.
- *Shinab.* King of Admah.
- *Shemeber.* King of Zeboyim.
- Some poor guy who doesn't even get a name but is the king of a place called Bela.

Moses introduces these two royal factions at war. The Promised Ones used to work for Kedorlaomer, the leader of the Monarchs, but they rebelled. Maybe they didn't like the hours. Maybe they wanted better benefits. How did Kedorlaomer respond? Well, Moses first tells us that the Monarchs killed lots of other people for no articulated reason (14:4–7). Perhaps they were distracted by other skirmishes, so they couldn't give their attention to the betrayal of the Promised Ones.

The climax comes in 14:8–9 as the two factions finally meet for battle in the Valley of Siddim. Though it's "four kings against five," the Monarchs don't seem to be the underdogs, because Moses has just narrated their bloody streak of success.

Moses' storytelling would likely frustrate modern readers because he fades to black before the first sword is drawn. We get no killing, only comedy. Because in the next scene, the Promised Ones—or at least their two most prominent players from Sodom and Gomorrah—borrow a battle tactic from Monty Python's King Arthur and "Run away!" Some make it to the hills, while others fall into the Valley of Siddim's pesky tar pits.

The Monarchs plunder the kings of Sodom and Gomorrah and then go home. Oh, and then we get this detail, as if Moses finally remembers why he's telling us all this: "They also carried off Abram's nephew Lot and his possessions, since he was living in Sodom" (14:12). Lot once lived "near" wickedness (13:12), now he lives "in" it. Again: uh-oh.

With this piece of news, we're thankful that Abram and Sarai don't whittle their days away at bingo and bocce ball. It's one thing if the Monarchs are skipping through Abram's neighborhood. But now they've kidnapped his nephew. They must do something about this!

Wait. Hang on a second? Do we really think Abram's 318-man ATF is any match for these marauding Monarchs? I mean, these guys just wiped out the Rephaites in Ashteroth Karnaim. The Rephaites in Ashteroth Karnaim, I tell you! Okay, you probably don't know who these people are. But Moses does, and his friends who first read Genesis 14 do, too. Later in the Torah, he describes how Israel defeated Og, the King of Bashan, who was "the last of the Rephaites." Then he describes his bed. It "was decorated with iron and was more than nine cubits long and four cubits wide. It is still in Rabbah of the Ammonites" (Deut. 3:11).[12] That's eighteen feet long and six feet wide! This thing would make Shaq feel slight. Og definitely played center for some made-up ancient Near Eastern basketball team. And he was a Rephaite.

Just so we're clear, Abram and his militia are in hot pursuit of these undefeated giant slayers. Even the most optimistic reader can't

---

12. Thanks to Sam Emadi for making this connection in our conversation (*Bible Talk*, episode 4).

expect success. But the ATF win—and it's not close. They recover their possessions and their people and then return home (14:13–16). He rescues his stupid nephew (and will need to again). He's brave and puts his life on the line. Now, Moses doesn't linger on Abram's motivation. You might say he keeps it hidden. But the chapter's concluding episode explains how his kingly contemporaries understood what we just read.[13]

GENESIS 14:17–24 // A ROYAL (AND DIVINE?) TETE-A-TETE

By the time we get to the end of Genesis 14, it's pretty obvious that Abram is more like a king than a recluse. He makes royal alliances and receives royal company. First, he's greeted by the king of Sodom, who apparently survived the tar pit. Then he's approached by a new king from a new place: Melchizedek of Salem.[14]

Let's briefly rewind to one of the Lord's promises to Abram: "I will bless those who bless you, and whoever curses you I will curse" (12:3). This promise is the key to understanding this passage. Look at what happens with Melchizedek: he blesses Abram with bread, wine, and a prayer of thanks (14:18–20). Then Abram blesses him back by giving him "a tenth of everything" (14:20). *I will bless those who bless you.* Where on earth did this guy come from? We don't know. But we do

---

13. For similar passages of men using 300ish conquering heroes to crush God's enemies, check out Judges 6–8 and 1 Samuel 30.

14. Psalm 110 and Hebrews 5–7 have all sorts of things to say about this guy. In fact, Sam argues that Psalm 110 is in direct conversation with Genesis 14. While waxing eloquent about this future priest-king who will come from the order of Melchizedek, David mentions that he will "crush kings on the day of his wrath . . . crushing the rulers of the whole earth" (110:5–6). That's exactly what Abram does in Genesis 14! What's more, that word *rulers* could also be translated "head." So you could argue that David reads Genesis 14 and sees Abram as a serpent crusher, thus fulfilling Gen. 3:15. But David also sees in the future another priest-king. Now Jim on the passage: "Abram's conquest and Melchizedek's royal priesthood will be realized in the future king that God has promised to raise up from David's line." Read the psalm and check out the connections for yourself. (Again: *Bible Talk*, episode 4).

know he's joined Abram in the worship of the Lord and, as a result, has received both Abram's and the Lord's blessing.[15]

The king of Sodom? Well, he takes a different path. The last time we saw him he was hightailing it out of the Valley of Siddim to get away from Kedorlaomer. He made it out alive but lost everything in the process. Thankfully, Abram got the king's stuff back, which likely explains why he's so eager to chat. Did you notice how he jumps straight to his request: "Give me the people and keep the goods for yourself" (14:21)?

Maybe the king of Sodom knows what happened with Melchizedek and he's trying to get in Abram's good graces. *No, no, no, I'm not like that greedy king. Keep the goods for yourself. You deserve them!* Or maybe he's nervous about the future of his kingdom. He knows his future depends not on goods that can grow back but on people who can make the goods grow back. We don't know his motivation. But compared with the previous conversation, one element is conspicuously missing: the Lord. This king's eyes aren't looking up at the creator of heaven and earth; they're looking around at the tenuous state of his money, his manpower, and his military alliances.

Abram rejects this arrangement. "Not so fast," he says. "That's not how this works. The Lord demands that I take nothing from you so that you don't steal glory from him" (14:22–24). Abram trusts that he will receive the land because the Lord has given it to him, not because he's in some special arrangement with another untrustworthy, unsavory king. *I will bless those who bless you, and whoever curses you I will curse.* The king of Sodom has "cursed" Abram by tempting him to place just a little bit of his confidence in his position and possessions, however well deserved they might be. And if you know the story, it won't be long before that curse is returned to him.

In Genesis 12–14, Abram has made progress in trusting God's promises. He didn't start off well (12:10–20) but has since resisted the

---

15. Moses puts on the lips of both Melchizedek and Abram the same honorific about the Lord: "God Most High, Possessor of heaven and earth" (14:19, 22 ESV). They're "speaking the same language" because they're worshiping the same God.

allure of both a return to Egypt and a wrongheaded relationship with the king of Sodom. He really does believe in the promises of God, and this belief is proof of his righteousness (15:6). Moses, meanwhile, has charted the first moments of God's promises coming to fruition: those who have blessed Abram have been blessed, and those who have cursed Abram have been cursed—or at least they've secured their cursing appointment.

God's doing exactly what he said he would do through Abram and Sarai. And yet they still don't have a son. This absence becomes the emphasis of the next episode of Abram's life.

SIX

GENESIS 15-17

> I, the undersigned, shall forfeit all rights, privileges, and licenses herein and herein contained, et cetera, et cetera . . . *fax mentis incendium gloria culpum, et cetera, et cetera . . . memo bis punitor delicatum*! It's all there, black and white.
>
> —WILLY WONKA, READING THE FINE PRINT

> Took a tour to see the stars
> But they weren't out tonight
> —PHOEBE BRIDGERS, "CHINESE SATELLITE"

We all break promises sometimes.

I promised my wife I'd do the dishes before bed, but I forgot. I promised a church member I'd give her feedback on a teaching outline, but that was months ago—and I still haven't looked at it. I promised Johnny I would throw football with him "in just a few minutes," but I kept finding one thing after another I "had to do." I promised my daughter Zoë she would be disciplined if her defiance persisted, but I lost heart. I promised my daughter Elliot I would jump off the diving board at least one time last summer, but Labor Day came and went and I never found the time or got the nerve. She reminded me of this the day the pool closed for the season.

We oversleep, we double-book, we show up late. We tell someone we won't tell anyone anything, but we whisper to someone else if they promise not to tell. We run into an old friend and say, "Let's get together!" but we know we'll never initiate. Some fictions are so ordinary. Others are world shattering. Marriages soberly and eagerly entered into before a crowd of smiling friends are crushed under a pile of "irreconcilable differences." Kids wait on doorsteps, listening for rattling engines that never come; they sit by phones that never ring.

Our unread emails and overlooked texts collect our most recent and well-meaning failures. Our kids and loved ones carry our most egregious. God help us. We all break promises sometimes.

Thankfully, the Lord is "not like man"; he never lies (Num. 23:19). On our good days, we believe this. We really do. But sometimes, we're tired from a slew of bad days. Sometimes, circumstances pile up and prosecute our faith. And, if we're honest, we begin to wonder if they're presenting compelling evidence.

In Genesis 15–17, we watch Abram and Sarai endure both good days and bad.

GENESIS 15 // THE LORD'S COVENANT CEREMONY (IN TWO PARTS)

PART 1: GENESIS 15:1-8

When we meet Abram at the beginning of Genesis 15, he's thumbing through some circumstantial evidence. He's looking at God's promises and then he's looking at his life and he sees less overlap than he expected. Though the Lord promised him a home and a son, he's still more or less a childless nomad. His heir is a servant, not a son. He still has to fight off parades of pirate-kings like we just saw in Genesis 14.

After some time passes (15:1),[1] the Lord brings up the controversial topic himself. He tells Abram that he is as dependable as a shield, which causes Abram to gush with uncertainty. I have no kid, he says (15:2–3). A bit later, he frets about the land: How do I know I'll actually inherit this land? How do I know I can trust you (15:8)? The rest of Genesis 15 answers these questions with a short field trip followed by an elaborate demonstration.

The field trip happens in 15:5 after the Lord reassures Abram he has nothing to worry about. Then, like Rafiki to Simba, he leads Abram outside and tells him to look up at the sky. But unlike Rafiki to Simba, the Lord tells Abram not to "remember who you are" but to "remember who I am."[2] The Lord gives Abram no evidence apart from his undivided attention. In fact, he doubles down on the difficulty of his promises by saying he won't just give Abram offspring that will become a great nation, he'll give Abram so many offspring that he won't even be able to number them.

After this comes the culmination of Moses' portrait of Abram so far: "Abram believed the LORD, and he credited it to him as righteousness" (15:6). What a significant comment, one that receives ample attention in the New Testament.[3] But for now, it's worth noting two things:

- *Abram's faith.* He believed God's word *before* its fulfillment. This is the narrative version of the principle that faith is "assurance about what we do not see" (Heb. 11:1).
- *The Lord's accounting.* The Lord *credits* Abram as righteous. The righteousness the Lord grants to Abram comes not as a wage but as a gift. Which means it comes from the outside, not the inside. It's alien, not inherent. Abram is righteous not because of

---

1. Abram was seventy-five in 12:4, eighty-six in 16:16, and ninety-nine in 17:1. While we don't know exactly how much time has passed by the beginning of Genesis 15, it's safe to say that it's at least a few years.

2. Okay, technically Mufasa's ghost tells Simba this. But you get the point.

3. A few highlights: Rom. 4:20–24; Gal. 3:6; James 2:23.

all the good things he has done—which should be obvious from what we've already read and will become more obvious with what we're about to read. Abram is righteous because the Lord has graciously declared him so on account of his faith.[4]

So that's the field trip. Notice how God concludes the first part of his argument: "I am the LORD, who brought you out of . . ." If I stopped the sentence there and asked you to fill in the blank with its ending, I wonder whether you'd write down "Egypt." A defensible answer. After all, that's how the Lord talks about himself during his preamble before the Ten Commandments. But here, he says, "I am the LORD, who brought you out of Ur of the Chaldeans to give you this land to take possession of it" (15:7). Here's Moses' point: just as God will one day save all of Israel, he has already saved the first Israelite.

But that first Israelite is still dealing with a gnawing question: "Lord, how can I know for sure that you're trustworthy?" You're about to read a bizarre, one-act play that answers this question. It's as if the Lord tells Abram, "Okay, though my word should be sufficient for your faith, I'll give you something more."

PART 2: GENESIS 15:9-20

When you first read this passage, I suspect you closed your Bible and said something like, "Okay, then." It is, admittedly, quite weird. It's unfamiliar. But just because it's unfamiliar to us doesn't mean it's nonsense. Imagine we somehow plopped Abram down into this year's Kentucky Derby. Or at the starting line of a Tough Mudder. He'd have lots of questions, but we could explain to him what was going on.[5]

---

4. The New Testament sheds a bit of light on where belief like this comes from: it comes from God, "so that no one can boast" (Eph. 2:9). While Moses doesn't make this theological truth part of his text, the subtext of the whole Bible is that salvation always comes at God's initiative and is the result of God's grace.

5. Well, if it were a Tough Mudder, *you* would have to explain to him what's going on, because I wouldn't be able to.

So let me attempt to do that. These verses describe a covenant ceremony. It's a two-scene, one-act play. In scene 1, Abram builds a road. But instead of using asphalt and iron, he uses split-up cows, goats, and rams, along with a few birds, which he for some reason keeps intact. After this bloody construction project, the Lord knocks him out[6] and then gives an ominous, spoiler-ridden soliloquy about Israel's future.

Did you catch what the Lord said about Israel? Let's not forget the question this whole spectacle is supposed to be answering: How do I know I can trust you about this land? So far, the Lord "reassured" Abram by putting him to sleep and then telling no one in particular that his descendants will be estranged slaves in a country "not their own." Oh, and it will be this way *for four hundred years!* Script doctors would have a field day with Moses' depressing plot. But there's good news here, too: the Lord also promises that he will one day punish these enslavers and enrich Abram's descendants in the process. This will all begin well after Abram is in the grave (15:15), and it won't end until the time is right (15:16).[7]

If I could summarize the Lord's promise to Abram in a slightly wordy compound sentence that kind of cheats because it uses an em-dash: even though my promise will seem precarious for a really, really long time, you have nothing to worry about because I'm totally good— and I'm totally in control.

So scene 1 concludes with a rousing speech from the Lord while our protagonist snores nearby. We still hear him snoring when the curtain comes up for scene 2.

It's dark and getting darker. After a while, we can no longer see the bloody appendages that double as guardrails for the short road. After

---

6. Which reminds us of the "deep sleep" that the Lord caused to come over Adam before he established another covenant, the covenant of marriage.

7. That enigmatic phrase about the Amorites is essentially saying, "Your descendants will return when your enemies' sin has outlasted my patience."

a longer while, we smell something before we can see it: it's smoke. Our eyes water at first and then burn. We finally see what's causing the smoke: a firepot and a blazing torch, side by side like eternal friends. They—surely there's a better word for this, right?—*walk* the road from end to end, from goat to pigeon and ram to dove. Once they get to the end, a disembodied voice thunders from above, "To your descendants I give this land."

And then the curtain falls yet again. End scene. The pot and the torch bow center-stage. We're afraid to throw flowers at them; it might cause the theater to burn down. So we just clap. That's it. That's the Lord's one-act covenant ceremony.

So what's it mean? At this point, you're wondering whether this whole thing is just a bit too avant-garde, an esoteric piece of abstract art with a question-begging title: *Will You Trust Me?* By God. But don't worry, this is just an ancient Near Eastern Tough Mudder. We can grasp it with a bit of effort and explanation.

Today, when two parties make a covenant,[8] they pay lots of different people—lawyers, loan officers, notaries, etcetera—lots of money to tell them where to sign on lots of pieces of paper. Sometimes, such covenants are followed by a ceremony, such as taking an Instagram photo with your realtor or ringing the bell on the New York Stock Exchange. Several thousand years ago, when two parties made a covenant, they didn't have lawyers to pay or papers to sign. So to solemnify their agreement, they would engage in a covenant-binding ceremony like the one we just read in Genesis 15. Both parties would walk the bloody road. In doing so, they would be saying to each other and to everyone else, "If I fail to keep the terms of this covenant, then let what's happened to these animals happen to me."[9]

---

8. My working definition of *covenant*: mutual promises that assume blessings for faithfulness and curses for unfaithfulness.

9. Jer. 34:18 alludes to this. The Lord promises to judge Israel's priests because they have failed to keep the terms of the covenant.

So that's the basic framework. Now let's think about it in context. In Genesis 12:1–3, the Lord put forward the terms of agreement and bound the two parties—the Lord and Abram—together by word. Genesis 15:9–20 binds the same two parties together by deed. Now, what words does Abram say in Genesis 12? None. Moses simply reports, "So Abram went" (12:4). Similarly, what does Abram do in Genesis 15? Apart from some stage design, nothing. He's snoring. In both cases, the Lord initiates contact with Abram, and in both cases Abram is a passive yet blessed recipient.

If my reconstruction is accurate, then audiences who aren't dealing with cultural static like we are would have expected both parties to show up during scene 2. Remember, if both parties agree, then they must both walk the bloody road. But what do we get? Or, to be precise, *who* do we get? We only get the Lord. He's the smoking firepot and the blazing torch.[10] He's the one who—all by himself—passes between the pieces, saying to himself and to all creation, "If I fail to keep the terms of this covenant, then let what's happened to these animals happen to me." Or, put another way, "If I lie, you can kill me."

We all break promises sometimes. Will you, Lord? That's the question Abram asks at the beginning of Genesis 15. Scripture's answer so far, even just fifteen chapters in, is a confident, unequivocal, static-free no. He isn't Willy Wonka; we don't have to read the fine print. He's told us who he is, he's shown us who he is, and we can trust him. Even glimpses of the Lord ought to inspire lifelong faith.

On our good days, like I said, we believe this. We really do. But what do we do when the bad days come, when the smoke and fire of the Lord's presence is gone and all that surrounds us are foggy circumstances and fading promises?

Abram and Sarai are about to face a day like that.

---

10. It won't be long before these images are more directly tied to the Lord's presence. See, for example, Ex. 19:18.

GENESIS 16 // ABRAM AND SARAI'S COVENANT SCHEME

Sometimes, when bad days come, we sin. Overcome by stupidity or sadness or some cocktail of the two, we reinterpret God's past faithfulness as tortuous. We confuse his patience with cruelty. We doubt him and instead trust ourselves—and then things really start to go south. Genesis 16 is all this and more. It's stupidly sad and sadly stupid.

If the previous chapter confronted us with unusual furniture that required some assembly and examination—is that a chaise lounge or an ergonomically adventurous massage chair?—then this chapter delivers an IKEA box to our front door. No assembly required. Its details may be more tawdry and terrible than we're used to. But we're all familiar with the hell that gets unleashed when someone decides, once and for all, to take things into their own hands. In Genesis 16, Abram and Sarai pursue unrighteousness with religious fervor and all the while wonder whether the Lord is unrighteous. I wonder if this is familiar to you.

Moses wants us to see something else familiar, too. He wants us to see Adam and Eve in Abram and Sarai. Consider these connections between Genesis 16 and Genesis 3:

- When the Lord curses Adam for his sin, here's how he begins: "Because you have listened to the voice of your wife . . ." (3:17 ESV).[11] Notice how Moses describes Abram's behavior once Sarai

---

11. I can imagine some readers freaking out right now and saying, "This guy just said it's a sin to listen to your wife! Chauvinist! Complementarian! Sinner!" Well, two of those three would be true, but that's not what I'm saying. Of course it would be a sin to listen to your wife *when she's tempting you to sin.* That's obvious. But more than that, we need to remember what the Lord said about marriage after the fall. It will now be cursed with rivalry and the abuse of authority. Interestingly, Abram and Sarai are the first married couple Moses has spent any time with. So it shouldn't surprise us that their relationship shows evidence for the paradigmatic curses for men and women in marriage. Abram sinfully lorded his authority over his wife when he gave her to Pharaoh. Sarai sinfully took initiative and led her husband into sin with this covenant-breaking scheme. (Something similar happens in Genesis 19, where Lot is sinfully passive and so his daughters take sinful initiative.)

unhatches her sinful plot: "Abram listened to the voice of Sarai" (16:2 ESV).

- Here's how Moses describes the progression of Eve's activity in the garden: "She saw [the fruit] . . . took [it] . . . gave some to her husband . . . and he ate" (3:6). Notice also how he describes the progression of Sarai's activity in Canaan: "[She] took Hagar . . . and gave her to Abram her husband. . . . And he went in to Hagar" (16:3–4 ESV). Just like Eve's, Sarai's self-centered scheme provoked her husband to feast on something that never belonged to him, to make a choice that would yield disastrous consequences.[12]

- These last three connections aren't linguistic but thematic. First, in both cases, the pleasure is short lived. (Compare 3:7 with the last half of 16:4.) Second, in both cases, the guilty parties shift blame before they repent. (Compare 3:12–13 with 16:5.) Third, in both cases, someone is exiled (3:24; 16:6).

The fallout is as bad as the fornication. Hagar, when she finds out she's pregnant, immediately despises Sarai. Perhaps she feels used by her, and rightly so. It's not clear why. But Hagar's disdain for this family runs deep, as we'll see in later chapters. Sarai, meanwhile, goes ballistic and blames her husband. And her husband—passive as ever—is basically like, "Um, no, thanks, I'm staying out of this."[13] So Sarai makes Hagar's life impossible until she flees *while pregnant!* Everyone loses.

Did you notice who's conspicuously absent from Genesis 16:1–6? God. The smoke and fire have cleared and all that's left are sad, scheming sinners. All that changes in Genesis 16:7 when the angel of the

---

12. As Jim said in our conversation, Abram here is no better than Pharaoh. He's willing to take an Egyptian woman into his bed to satisfy himself (*Bible Talk*, episode 5).

13. Again, notice the paradigmatic temptations for husbands and wives in play here. Sarai wants to lord over her husband. Abram fails to wield his authority lovingly over his wife. Whereas in Genesis 12 Abram's sin was the abuse of authority, here his sin is his failure to use his authority at all.

Lord shows up.[14] For the rest of Genesis 16, the Lord is cleaning up their mess. He pursues Hagar with a series of questions,[15] and then he makes promises and predictions that diverge from the promises and predictions he's made about Abram.

The lesser promise shows up in 16:10: "I will surely multiply your offspring so that they cannot be numbered for multitude" (ESV). This is a common-grace promise. It will persist because of natural biology, not special blessing.[16] If the Lord promises Abram land, seed, and blessing, then his promise to Hagar of undifferentiated seed is paltry by comparison.[17]

The lesser prediction comes next (16:11–12). We've already seen how the Lord promised that Abram's seed will be a conduit of blessing the whole world. Okay, so that's a high bar. I'm not sure even the most optimistic mother would expect that of her son. So what does the Lord have in store for this other son of Abram? Will he be a blessing to the whole nation? Nope. The whole region? Nope. The whole zip code? Nope. The whole neighborhood? Nope. The cul-de-sac? Nope. C'mon, can he at least bless his roommates! Nope, a promise of blessing never comes.

The Lord has heard Hagar's misery, and he will continue to hear it, because her son, Ishmael, will be miserable. The Lord's prophecy never relents. There's not a single spark of hope. Ishmael will be stubborn and uncontrolled, cantankerous and disliked. Far from blessing the world, he will instead be the father of Israel's enemies.

This situation is awful. Abram's pregnant servant is on the run

---

14. Lots of ink has been spilled on who this guy is. A preincarnate Christ? An angel? Something else? I'm convinced it's an angel, though reasonable minds differ. A similar complication shows up at the beginning of Genesis 18, and that one is even trickier.

15. Another echo of Genesis 3. Compare 16:8 and 3:9.

16. Abram himself seems to get this in 17:18. Ishmael is his flesh-and-blood, common-grace, blessings-free son. Later in the New Testament (Gal. 4:28–30), Paul will refer to Ishmael as a "son born according to the flesh." The promises Jesus secured for his people run not through Ishmael but through Isaac, the "son born by the power of the Spirit."

17. In the next chapter, the Lord will grant nationhood to Ishmael's offspring, but the contrast persists: Isaac's inheritance is blessed and Ishmael's is not. Ishmael gets kids, but not the covenant (17:20).

because he and his wife are selfish. They've ignored the Lord, and their manmade scheme to bring about blessing has brought only heartbreak. Hagar doesn't deserve this. No one is looking out for her. No one sees her. No one hears her. No one except the Lord.

This isn't the end of Hagar's story. But it also isn't a conversion experience. We don't quite know yet what Hagar thinks of Israel's God. (Remember, she's from Egypt.) We don't quite know yet whether this interaction changes the course of her life forever, or just for a season. We'll have a better sense of all this when we get to Genesis 21. But for now, we do know for certain that the Lord hears and sees and speaks to and cares for all people. (*Ishmael* means "God hears.")

Despite the Lord's reassertions, despite his elaborate demonstration of his trustworthiness, a torrent of unexpected circumstances have eroded Abram and Sarai's faith. The barren months have taken their toll. But circumstances are never determinative, they're revelatory. They're thermometers, not thermostats. They reveal what's in a heart, and Abram and Sarai's hearts have become as cold as ice, crying out within themselves a stubborn question that they'd previously swatted away: Can we really trust the Lord?

In Genesis 15, the Lord yells yes. In Genesis 16, the Lord's people yell no. You might wonder whether we're about to get another restart. Isn't he tired of these faithless people?

This time, the Lord is the one who answers no.

GENESIS 17 // THE LORD'S COVENANT SIGNS

Like Jerry Seinfeld's neighbor Kramer, God tends to show up unannounced and uninvited. When he crashes through the door—as in 12:1, 15:1, and now 17:1—something significant is about to happen. Even after all these years, the Lord hasn't given up on these people. By now, Abram is almost a century old; twelve years have passed since his botched plan with Hagar. He's been walking with the Lord for nearly a quarter century (12:4). And now, finally, the time has come for the Lord to make good on his promises.

In 17:1–8, the Lord reiterates the high points of his promises to Abram and adds a few special details:

- "Your name will be Abraham" (17:5).
- "Kings will come from you" (17:6). This has been alluded to and perhaps assumed, but now the Lord makes this element of the promise explicit.
- "I will establish my covenant as an *everlasting* covenant" (17:7).[18] Again, this wouldn't have come across as a huge shock. How could "all the nations of the earth" be blessed through Abram, but only for a while?

The rest is boilerplate blessedness.

Now, normally, when God speaks to Abram, he talks about what he has done or is doing or will one day do for him. But in 17:9–14, he flips the script and explains what this new man named Abraham must do for him, what it looks like to walk faithfully before him (17:1). And his explanation is a bit surprising.

For Abraham, faithfulness means circumcision for every man among them, forever. From Ishmael to his servants to his herdsmen to his servants' and herdsmen's kids to the 318 members of the ATF—they must all go under the knife, and the consequence for refusal is dire. If you don't cut off a little bit, then you'll be cut off all the way. Or, put another way, the wages of skin is death (17:14). Hopefully you can see why this particular test of faithfulness would be nerve-wracking for Abraham. A mere slip of the knife would mean no promised son.

The Lord had already pledged his commitment to Abraham with word and deed, smoke and fire. He had walked the bloody road himself.

---

18. The only explicitly everlasting covenant we've seen so far is with Noah in 9:16.

Now Abraham must pledge his own commitment to the Lord. And to do so, he must be willing to shed at least a little bit of blood. Though he was speechless in Genesis 12 and asleep in Genesis 15, now he must act in faith.[19]

Before we see how Abraham responds, Moses tells us that the Lord changes Sarai's name, too. As it turns out, both Abraham and Sarah receive a sign in this passage. His is approximately a million times more painful—for once, the man gets the more painful lot!—but both signs stick with them for life.

As the Lord audaciously dusts off these old promises, Abraham can't help but fall down and laugh.[20] But his isn't a laugh of mockery, it's a laugh of pent-up expectation, like watching a magician set up his grand finale and turning to a friend and saying, "How in the world is he going to pull this off?"

For twenty-five years, the Lord has walked alongside Abraham and proven himself to be trustworthy. Even as he has withheld fulfilling certain promises, he's never been unclear or capricious. And now it's time for the long-awaited reveal: your son has a name—Isaac—and a due date—"this time next year" (17:21).

What joy! What relief! What incredible, spectacular, perfect timing.

We all break promises sometimes. But the Lord never does. He's trustworthy, so trustworthy that a ninety-nine-year-old man would drop everything he was doing to circumcise himself and all of his friends to demonstrate his faith.

---

19. Though when the time came, I bet he wished he was still speechless and asleep!

20. Sarah also laughs when she hears the same news. We'll talk about that in the next chapter.

SEVEN

GENESIS 18-21

Long my imprisoned spirit lay
Fast bound in sin and nature's night;
Thine eye diffused a quickening ray,
I woke, the dungeon flamed with light;
My chains fell off, my heart was free;
I rose, went forth, and followed Thee.

–CHARLES WESLEY, "AND CAN IT BE?"

Evil societies always destroy their consciences.

–JAMES L. FARMER JR., FRIEND OF MARTIN LUTHER KING JR.

So far, we've had a front-row seat to Abraham's yo-yoing relation-ship with the Lord. He believes the Lord's promises; he tries to short-circuit the Lord's procrastination. He follows his wife into sin; he leads his household into obedience. He's counted as righteous by God; he's cold and uncaring toward Hagar. After Genesis 15–17's mesmer-izing covenant ceremony and failed covenant scheme and successful covenant sign, we might expect the long-awaited birth of the covenant son—or, at least for Abraham, some covenant convalescing.

But that's not what happens. In Genesis 18–20, Moses charts our principal characters' up-and-down behavior—first Sarah's, then our old friend Lot's, and then Abraham's. Though Sarah and Abraham have new names, they still struggle with the same old sins. Though Lot has repeatedly been on the receiving end of God's mercy, he can't kick his attraction to the world.

GENESIS 18:1-15 // A DIVINE DINNER PARTY

One question springs to mind after reading the first half of this chapter: Who are these three mysterious vistitors?

They are angelic messengers who stand for and speak on behalf of the Lord, at least until he chooses to speak for himself. That doesn't mean their names are Father, Son, and Spirit. These men aren't a deconstructed apparition of the triune God. They merely represent him, so we can say, along with Moses, that the Lord appeared and spoke to Abraham through them (18:1, 13, 17, 22).

We know they're not mere mortals because of how Abraham acts:

- He bows to the ground, and they do not refuse the honor (18:2).
- He places himself under their authority as servant to lord, not peer to peer (18:3).
- He shows them lavish hospitality (18:4–8)—more on that later, as hospitality becomes an important theme in these chapters.

In Genesis 18:1–8, Abraham and Sarah host a dinner party with these divine guests that sets up yet another divine interruption and yet another reaffirmation of divine promises (18:9–15). The repetition might make you wonder why Moses is taking such a roundabout way to his destination. Is he lost? No, a masterful storyteller can never be lost, just like your dad can never be lost, even after he's made his third U-turn in as many minutes.

A few observations about this conversation between Abraham, Sarah, and the Lord. First, notice that Sarah responds to God's reassertion of his faithfulness just like her husband did: with a laugh (18:12).

Second, notice *why* the Lord's faithfulness is so funny to Sarah. She laughs because she knows where babies come from—or she knows *how* babies come from where they come from. She laughs because she knows that she and her husband simply no longer have working equipment; their software can no longer run the necessary programs. Moses tells us as much: "Sarah was past the age of childbearing" (18:11). Sarah seems to tell us as much about her husband: "After I am worn out and my lord is old, will I now have this pleasure?" (18:12). The biological clock has run out on both Sarah and Abraham. It appears Moses is a modest storyteller, too.[1]

Third, notice the details of the back-and-forth. From the very beginning, the Lord makes his conversation with Abraham about Sarah (18:9). You could say he's not really talking to Abraham at all but *through* Abraham to Sarah. Of course, the Lord's the only one aware of what he's up to. Abraham's probably wondering why he's repeating himself. Sarah, meanwhile, assumes she's hidden, eavesdropping on her husband and laughing "to herself" (18:12). But as Hagar taught us, the Lord hears everything. After he asks Abraham about Sarah's secret laugh, the conversation crescendos into a reaffirmation of his faithfulness (18:13–14). This causes Sarah to emerge from the entrance of the tent to defend herself—not with the truth but with a fearful lie.[2]

Moses portrays Isaac's upcoming birth not as a pleasant surprise

---

1. To be explicit about the subtext: Sarah was in menopause and Abraham could no longer bring "pleasure" to his wife. That's what Moses just modestly proposed. Yes, Abraham has other kids through his next wife, Keturah. But I'm inclined to read Moses' and Sarah's comments as proof that Isaac's birth required a biological miracle, reversing the effects of both menopause and impotence. First God made their union possible, and then he made it fruitful.

2. She laughs like her husband, and she lies like her husband.

but as a biological miracle. In doing so, the Lord shouts to Sarah what her husband has already believed: nothing is too hard for the Lord (18:14). Abraham heard of this faithfulness and laughed out of pent-up expectation. Sarah laughed out of pent-up frustration. No matter what, God is always faithful—sometimes miraculously so—even when we find the unfolding of his faithfulness to be so absurd, so glacial, so against the grain that we can't help but find it funny.

Abraham learned this lesson in Genesis 17. Now Sarah needed to come face to face with God's faithfulness—hence Genesis 18:1–15. This lesson was so important, in fact, that the Lord felt it necessary to interrupt a divine dinner party.

GENESIS 18:16–19:29 // A DIVINE DESTRUCTION + A DIVINE DELIVERANCE

Way back in Genesis 13, after Lot chose Sodom and Gomorrah because of their walkable neighborhoods and good schools, Moses told us the future: the Lord would destroy Sodom and Gomorrah because the people are wicked (13:10, 13). Now we get the full story, and it's framed by a pressing question: "Will not the Judge of all the earth do right?" (18:25).

The answer, of course, is that he will. He always does. This unambiguous affirmation protects us from misunderstanding. The back-and-forth conversation isn't between Abraham the Merciful and the Lord Who's Frothing at the Mouth. Far from it. The Lord is full of mercy, and Abraham's shrewd negotiation tactics can't squeeze out a few more drops. With each offer—fifty? forty-five? forty? thirty?—two things become clear. First, the Lord's purposes remain steadfast. Second, even as Abraham has rightly esteemed the Lord's commitment to justice, he has wrongly estimated Sodom and Gomorrah's commitment to sin. There aren't even ten righteous people there (18:32).

As the story unfolds, Moses tracks the whereabouts of Abraham and Sarah's divine dinner guests. He tells us they went toward Sodom not once but twice (18:16, 22). Though his camera lingers for a bit on that dispiriting negotiation, he quickly pans back to these guys as they arrive at Sodom (19:1). It's clear they have business with this place, and if we've paid attention, we know what kind of business it is.

Then there's a twist. Who do these divine representatives meet when they arrive? Our old friend Lot. Years go, Lot relocated east, toward a land that appeared to promise both the presence of God and the presents of the world.[3] For a while, he lives "among the cities of the plain" (13:12). Before long, he's captured by the Mesopotamian Monarchs. When Moses describes this ordeal, he adds that Lot was now "living in Sodom" (14:12). Then Lot blips off the radar for a few chapters until now, when we find him not only in Sodom but sitting at its gate.[4] Do you see the progression? Since his separation from Abraham, he's gone from Sodom's suburbs to Sodom's city hall.

Lot's shifting proximity toward Sodom's halls of power is significant. But we need to be careful not to overinterpret what Moses is doing here. Lot has indeed made a series of foolish, even sinful decisions to get where he is. And yet he remains a man of faith, fumbling his way toward righteousness in a town flooded by unrighteousness.

Maybe you're uncertain. Lot? Righteous? No way. But before you dismiss it, let's compare Genesis 19 and Genesis 18. Let's ask two questions: What's the same? What's different?

Here's what's the same:

- Angels show up (19:1).
- Lot, like Abraham, bows to the ground and places himself under their authority as lord to servant, not peer to peer (19:2).
- Lot, like Abraham, insists on showing his divine guests hospitality (19:3); they share a meal.

---

3. Me, a few chapters ago: "Lot wants the appearance of paradise with the Lord *and* the prosperity of this world."

4. Read Ps. 1:1. You might say Lot has not taken this advice.

Here's what's different:

- There are only two angels, not three.
- They initially reject his offer of hospitality.
- With Abraham, these divine guests ate like royalty: a tender calf, some curds, some baked bread made from the finest flour. With Lot, they ate like inmates: bread without yeast (19:3).

The similar setups offer a clue that we should read these passages in conversation with one another. Abraham is trying to be faithful in a place that looks like paradise. Where else do you dine with the divine under a tree (18:8)? Lot is trying to be faithful in a place that is about to look like hell. Where else do smoke and sulphur show up?

Despite Lot's terrible surroundings, he's genuinely trying to be faithful. He protects his visitors from the vile city square (19:2–3), he pleads with his wicked neighbors (19:6–7), he believes judgment is coming, and he tells his sons-in-law to hurry up and get out (19:14).

Yes, he also—*gulp*—offers his daughters to a detestable mob (19:8). He hesitates (19:16). He negotiates for a new place to live because he's so afraid (19:18–20).

We shouldn't let Lot off the hook for his behavior. He was mixed up. He should have known that the Lord didn't need his unrighteous scheme to accomplish his purposes. He should never have put one virtue—hospitality, even hospitality to the Lord's representatives—against another virtue—protecting his daughters.[5]

But Lot, like Abraham, is righteous. Yes, the New Testament tells us this (2 Peter 2:7). But Peter isn't just optimistically grasping at straws. He's reading Moses and basing his unambiguous conclusion on everything you and I have just read. After all, there's no "Part 2: Lot Goes to Seminary." The only other story we get about Lot makes him look worse than even his halfhearted departure from his hometown.

---

5. I'm grateful for Jim Hamilton's thoughts on this. *Bible Talk*, episode 6.

So what evidence does Moses give us that Lot is righteous?

First, Lot's like Abraham (sort of). We've already talked about this. In bowing and feeding and showing hospitality to his divine guests, in believing and acting on the Lord's promises, Lot mirrors Abraham. Yes, the reflection is dim. But he does what he can despite his awful circumstances—which plague him because of his past selfish decisions. If Abraham offers us an imperfect picture of life with God, then Lot offers us a picture of an imprisoned one.

Second, Lot lives. Who did the Lord promise to save from Sodom? The righteous ones. There weren't ten. But there were at least three, and the judge of all the earth has done what is right by them. Lot is alive, which means the Lord found him righteous.

Lot is righteous because of how he sees and how he hears. He sees the wickedness of his neighbors and wants to protect his divine guests. Meanwhile, his neighbors are blinded by their sin—both metaphorically and then for real (19:11). Lot also hears of the Lord's coming judgment and acts on it. Lot can see, and Lot can hear. He is righteous.

So is the lesson of Genesis 19 that righteous people see and hear and therefore you should see and hear to be righteous? Not at all. Sin plagues us all, and all sin is in some sense blinding rebellion. Sometimes that rebellion looks like the nauseating debauchery of these men of Sodom. You can see it, hear it, feel it—it makes you sick. They want to rape angels. Does it get any worse?

But blinding rebellion isn't always so, well, rebellious. Just look at Lot's wannabe sons-in-law. Their rebellion—their blindness to his trustworthiness; their deafness to the Lord's commands—didn't cause them to claw at the door of Lot's house, clamoring to get in so they could devour another man with their desire. It caused them to shrug their shoulders, to stifle a laugh, to indulge a sideways glance in the face of sincerity. Or, in the case of Lot's wife, to look one last time at the place she loved the most.

Genesis 19 demands that we take all sin seriously. Though the sins of the men of Sodom and the family of Lot look different—though the former's strike us as repellant and the latter's as more reasonable—they both provoke the same response: righteous judgment from the righteous judge of all the earth. He always does what is right.

And then there's Lot—blind and deaf compared with Abraham, blessed with the eyes and ears of a hawk compared with everyone else. What do we do with him? We rejoice that he lived. We rejoice that he is righteous not because of his relative morality but because of the Lord's righteous mercy.

This is Moses' argument, not mine. Did you catch it? "When he hesitated"—when he sinned!—"the men grasped his hand and the hands of his wife and of his two daughters and led them safely out of the city, for the LORD was merciful to them" (19:16). This is how divine deliverance always works. God plucks and protects whomever he wants whenever he wants from wherever they are. If Moses wanted to teach us that mercy is the prize of the moral, then Lot's salvation wouldn't make any sense. But Genesis 19 doesn't teach that: instead, it teaches the confounding lesson that mercy is the prize of the righteous, and the righteous are those whom the Lord has remembered (19:29), those who have received the gift of faith, even imperfect faith.

GENESIS 19:30-36 // LOT'S FINAL ACT

We've not yet discussed the second sordid tale of Genesis 19, where Lot gets raped by and impregnates his daughters (19:30–36). This is his final scene, Moses' closing act for this tragic man. Once encumbered by great possessions, Lot is now bereft and abused and alone. Once given the pride of place, he now lives in a cave and gets so drunk he doesn't even know what his children are doing to him.[6] His steps toward compromise have led him to a cavern of catastrophe.

---

6. Who does that remind you of? Flip to Genesis 9 for a reminder. In fact, Genesis 6–9 and Genesis 19 have a lot in common. See appendix 1 for a chart I got from Jim.

We began these chapters expecting a pregnancy. As they conclude, we find that Moses does indeed give us one, but it's not the one we've been waiting for and certainly not one we wanted.

I suspect Moses wrote Genesis 19:30–36 to underscore the lesson that Lot is righteous not because of his deeds but because of God's mercy. I also suspect Lot's daughters' scheme reminded him of Sarah's in Genesis 16. Like Sarah, they want to preserve their "old" father's family line. Seeing no options, they take their future into their own hands to disastrous effect. Hagar's son, Ishmael, becomes a perennial enemy to Moses and his countrymen (16:11–12). So do Lot's sons, who are also his grandsons. These boys become the patriarchs of two stubborn enemies: the Moabites and the Ammonites. We've already talked about the Ammonites—remember the Shaq-sized bed?—but the Moabites become problems, too. (See Deut. 23:3.)

And yet, despite all this awfulness, the Lord is up to something.

I've spent a lot of ink describing what Moses knows. And yet, every now and then, it's worth mentioning what he doesn't know. Or *who* he doesn't know. Moses doesn't know that Moab is also the ancestor of Ruth, a faithful Moabitess, and he doesn't know that Ruth is the great-great-grandmother of King David. In case it's not clear: No Moab, no Ruth. No Ruth, no King David. No King David, no King Jesus. Moses doesn't know this, but the seed of this incestuous abuse eventually flowers into the birth of the Savior.

GENESIS 20 // SISTER FIB 2: BACK IN THE HABIT

I wonder whether, while reading this chapter, you, like me, wanted to scream, *Abraham, what are you doing!* It's a fair question. Abraham has sinned in this exact same way already (12:10–20). He has even sinned in this exact same way after hearing the Lord affirm his promises and responding in obedience (12:1–9). How could he do it again?

Abraham has to be the only person who has sinned in the same way more than once. Right? *Right?*

We just spent some time comparing Lot to Abraham to see how Genesis 19 casts Lot in a positive, but dim, light. When we get to Genesis 20, it might seem obvious to compare Abraham to his former self, to talk about the foolishness of repeated sins. But instead I want to compare Abraham to the pagan king Abimelek.

Throughout the chapter, King Abimelek is at pains to reiterate his innocence. Though he "took" Sarah, he never touched her (20:2, 6). The Lord didn't let him (20:6).[7] Moses records these protestations to show us that God's promises are still intact. Abraham, meanwhile, is at pains to reiterate that he's only kind of a liar, and a condescending one at that (20:11–13).

By the end of the chapter, Abraham and Sarah leave and get richer in the process. The basic plot points of Genesis 20 align with Genesis 12:10–20.[8]

Why the repeated stories? To what end? Is this *Groundhog Day?* First, because Genesis 12:3 is coming to pass: those who bless Abraham will be blessed, and those who curse him will be cursed. We see this more clearly with Genesis 12's sequel in Genesis 20. While Abimelek probably felt cursed by Abraham at first, in the end the momentary cursing gives way to blessings (20:17–18).

Second, because we need to look at this story as the culmination of Genesis 18–20's surprising delay. After the mess of Genesis 16 and the expectation-building glory of Genesis 17, we get this? Story after story of sinners laughing and looking back and lying. Story after story of the Lord listening and leading and protecting. In Genesis 17, the Lord declared his sovereign goodness and grace. In Genesis 18–20, he demonstrated it. His purposes will always come to pass. Nothing

---

7. Not only that, the Lord had to intervene with a dream (20:3). Anything good that happens in this chapter, he miraculously initiates.

8. Abraham and Sarah arrive at a new place; Abraham lies; Sarah is given away; the Lord intervenes (with plagues or with dreams); Abraham and Sarah leave better off than when they arrived.

can thwart him, not our doubts or our laughs, not our sins both big and small. We saw that with Sarah and Lot in Genesis 18 and 19, and we've just now seen it again—somewhat unbelievably—with Abraham in Genesis 20.

The story of Genesis is not "God saves the good guys and gets the bad guys, so I gotta be a good guy and not a bad guy." It's more complicated than that. After all, this is a real story about real people who really lived. And real people—even those declared righteous, even those who are objects of mercy—are really complicated. In one chapter of their lives, they submit to sin; in another, they fight. Throughout it all, God's purposes and mercy march on.

GENESIS 21:1-21 // A TALE OF TWO SONS

A few chapters ago, I called Ishmael Abraham's "flesh-and-blood, common-grace, blessings-free son." Ishmael gets kids, but not the covenant. He gets breath, but not the blessing. He sires princes, but not kings. If Isaac is the recipient of undiluted promises—land, seed, and blessing—Ishmael receives diet, caffeine-free ones.

In Genesis 21, we're face to face with a tale of two sons. Moses finally gives us the joy of long-awaited fulfillment, and he couples it with the sorrow of long-expected disappointment. He gives us laughter and weeping, new life and near death, a birth and a banishment. Until now, Moses has cast Ishmael and Isaac in similar molds. But now their diverging futures take center-stage.

GENESIS 21:1-7 // A GOOD LAUGH

Respectfully, if I were writing the story of Isaac's birth, I would slow down. Genesis 21 is the climax of our Genesis 12 expectations. So I'd describe the moment Sarah discovered she was with child. I'd record the conversation she had with Abraham about the Lord's miraculous, even hilarious timing. I'd try to capture the tense scene of a nonagenarian giving birth—the nerves felt before, the pain during, and the elation afterward; the moment she finally heard the first cries of the baby boy who once made her laugh. The promised offspring—after a series of fits and starts, of faithful successes and sinful failures—is finally here.[9]

But Genesis 21:1–7 does none of that. Why? Because for Moses, Isaac's birth isn't primarily a story about a bone-tired mother or even a biological miracle. It's about the Lord keeping his word. Whatever he says, he does.[10] He is gracious and trustworthy and sovereign (21:1, 2, 4).

And guess what? Sarah finally gets it. So rather than laughing *at* the Lord all alone, she looks forward to the years ahead when, spurred on by a kind of bemused belief, she will laugh *with* others as they reflect on the Lord's miraculous sovereignty. Ha! Who would have thought? He's been faithful yet again.

GENESIS 21:8-21 // OH, NO, ANOTHER BAD LAUGH

When Ishmael laughs at his brother's party (21:9),[11] he reminds us of Nimrod and Cain and other faithless fellows we've met along the way. He mirrors his father's worst moments. But Moses has charted Abraham and Sarah's trajectory of trust. They've grown. They've changed. Ishmael and Hagar, it seems, have not. The point of Genesis 21's contrast is straightforward: the Lord delights to do unexpected things that make the faithful worship and the faithless laugh.

If you laughed at your teacher or your boss, you might get detention or a talking-to from HR, but you probably wouldn't be kicked out of school or banished to a basement boiler room like Ryan in *The Office*. So we might be tempted to think Abraham and Sarah overreacted. But Moses wants us to agree with what happens for a few reasons.

First, Sarah's stated motivation (21:10). She's not taking the

---

9. We expect this in large part because that's how many of our modern stories are told. We think of stories from the subjective narrator's point of view—where the "I" is the prominent voice. Moses isn't writing that way. He doesn't even write that way when he becomes a main character himself from Exodus through Deuteronomy.

10. Thanks to John Kimbell for this phrasing.

11. What the NIV translates in 21:9 as "mocking," the ESV translates as "laughing."

mockery personally; instead, she's sizing up Ishmael and Hagar and realizing that they want nothing to do with the Lord. Their disposition toward God and his promises threatens the son of promise.

Second, the Lord tells Abraham to listen to his wife's voice (21:12). She's assessed the situation correctly. We should also note that this is a curious command—no, not because it's a bad idea to listen to your wife. Husbands generally should listen to their wives![12] It's curious because Abraham's listening to his wife is why they're facing this problem in the first place (16:2; cf. 3:17). Yet more evidence showing us this couple's growth.

Third, the concluding details of the story prove that Hagar and Ishmael reject the Lord's program. But before we get there, we need to talk about Genesis 21:14–19. These verses are pathetic, like in the high-school theater-class sense of the word. That is, they're full of pathos, of emotion. How fascinating that Moses slows down here, with the blessings-free son, like we expected him to with Isaac's birth. You can see the sunset send-off between father and son. You can feel the weight on Hagar's shoulders as she carries all their earthly wares toward an unforgiving desert. You can see the confusion on the boy's sunburned face as his mother stows him away under a bush. You can hear both Ishmael and Hagar sobbing—they're only a football field apart, about to be separated forever by death.

Hagar has been in a similar situation before, fleeing from Abraham and Sarah and fearful for her life. The events of Genesis 21 are more dire than Genesis 16. But the solution is the same: the Lord needs to show up. And so he does (21:17; cf. 16:7). Though Hagar has to avert her eyes (21:16), the Lord's gaze never falters and his attention never wanes. He sees and hears their distress, and he intervenes.

The story ends when the Lord leads mother and son to a well of water. He restores their lives—for the second time, at least in Moses' retelling. Then he adds this final note. And when I say "final," I mean

---

12. Love you, Mel.

it.[13] We get nothing else about Hagar and Ishmael. Here's how Moses closes the loop on their story: "God was with the boy as he grew up. He lived in the desert and became an archer. While he was living in the Desert of Paran, his mother got a wife for him from Egypt" (21:20–21).

For nearly two decades, Hagar had a front-row seat to God's miraculous faithfulness. She'd seen how he delighted to have mercy on sinful people. She should have left the well and led her son back home. But she doesn't. Instead, she plants her family's future in a desert near Egypt. In doing so, she leaves the Lord behind.

Why? Who can say? Perhaps she never got over that her son wasn't the son of the promise. Perhaps her life of suffering made her cold and closed off to God's faithfulness. Perhaps she scorned the Lord's mercy on Sarah and Abraham. Perhaps she thought proximity to his promises was a good-enough substitute for participation in his promises.

But this much is clear in Genesis 21: the Lord hears the cries and sees the affliction of those (like Ishmael) who have been left behind and those (like Hagar) who are headed in the wrong direction. He provides for and protects them. He avails himself to them. You could argue that at the end of Ishmael's story, he gets two-thirds of land, seed, and blessing. His offspring (seed) will become a great nation (21:13, 18), which implies land. The main difference between these two sons is that the Lord says there will be no blessing *through* Ishmael. That doesn't mean there's no blessing *for* Ishmael.

How tragic. To be so near and yet so far away, to enjoy the Lord's protection and provision while rejecting his promises.

GENESIS 21:22-33 // ABRAHAM THE ALIEN

We move from the height of drama to an idiosyncratic conversation about who owns a certain well. While this transition may seem confusing,

---

13. Though Ishmael does manage to make it to his dad's funeral (25:9).

don't let it vex you. Remember: the overriding promise in Moses' retelling of Abraham's life is that the Lord has promised him land, seed, and blessing. We've spent lots of time covering the question of seed and blessing. That's more or less been resolved—at least for now—through Isaac. But what about the land? Is Abraham still a wandering nomad? This question becomes more prominent in the pages to come.

For now, the answer is yes. King Abimelek says as much when he and Abraham strike up a treaty: "Show to me and the country where you *now reside as a foreigner* . . ." (21:23). In other words, you're welcome here—and you've been welcome here since you lied to me about your wife (Genesis 20)—but this is not your home.

Abraham doesn't dispute his alien status, but he does dispute his landlord's lackeys taking what isn't theirs—in this case, a well he dug himself. Abimelek claims ignorance and accepts Abraham's down payment of seven lambs. It's not exactly equivalent to paying three month's rent, but it's not far off. Abraham is acting in good faith because he knows he's still a squatter in rented space, an alien in a foreign land. Even after the treaty gets established—which further extends Abraham's commitment to bless those who bless him—the best Abraham can do is sign a long-term rental and spruce up the place with a tamarisk tree (21:33).

We'll return in a few chapters to a longer discourse on the unresolved question of land. But first, we must slow down because Moses' story is about to take its most surprising turn yet.

EIGHT

GENESIS 22

It was unthinkable that I would not follow orders.

–ADOLF EICHMANN

The reason my Father loves me is that I lay down my life—
only to take it up again. No one takes it from me, but I lay
it down of my own accord. I have authority to lay it down
and authority to take it up again. This command I received
from my Father.

–JESUS

Some folks really hate the Bible.[1] Atheist Richard Dawkins is among
them. Now, if we pressed him, I bet we'd find out that Dawkins
can handle some parts of the Bible, particularly when Jesus jibes with
Dawkins' own more "modern" sensibilities. But for Dawkins, these
benign blips are incidental to the entire Christian project, which he
finds both tawdry and contemptuous, beautiful to no one but the naive

---

1. This chapter has been adapted from the following article: Alex Duke, "Kill Your Son,
Abraham: Making Sense of a Shocking Command," Gospel Coalition, January 28, 2021, www
.thegospelcoalition.org/article/kill-son-shocking-command/.

Neanderthals who have accidentally survived into the twenty-first century.

I find all this funny because some folks, myself included, really love the Bible. If you've made it this far in this book, I suspect that's you, too. And you don't just love parts of it, you love every single word, even those that confuse and confound you. And you aren't a Neanderthal. You're just a normal Christian.

One part of the Bible normal people really love is a part that Dawkins really hates: Genesis 22, where Abraham follows God's orders and offers up his son Isaac as a sacrifice. It's a profoundly beautiful story, one marked by a father's love for his son, a son's trust in his father, and a promised blessing being passed down from one generation to the next.

Dawkins, um, disagrees:

> God ordered Abraham to make a burnt offering of his longed-for son. Abraham built an altar, put firewood upon it, and trussed Isaac up on top of the wood. His murdering knife was already in his hand when an angel dramatically intervened with the news of a last-minute change of plan: God was only joking after all, "tempting" Abraham, and testing his faith. A modern moralist cannot help but wonder how a child could ever recover from such a psychological trauma. By the standards of modern morality, this disgraceful story is an example simultaneously of child abuse, bullying in two asymmetrical power relationships, and the first recorded use of the Nuremberg defense: "I was only obeying orders."[2]

Yikes, Dr. Dawkins, tell us how you really feel!

But hang on. On the surface, all this frothing may seem reasonable. After all, I've just spent thousands of words defending the Lord's faithfulness. With Isaac's birth, he made good on his promises to Abraham

---

2. Richard Dawkins, *The God Delusion*.

and Sarah. So after all this, how in the world can his request to kill Isaac make moral or theological sense?

I suspect many Christians have silently wondered some version of this question. Genesis 22 is, admittedly, a shocking turn of events. But once we look closely at this passage, we'll realize that it doesn't villainize, it actually vindicates the Lord.

Let's slow down and look at a few things we might have missed.

1. Moses frames these events as a test (22:1). The main thing you should take away from Genesis 22:1 is that word *tested*. Moses doesn't say God punished Abraham or that he tempted Abraham. He says that God tested Abraham. Dawkins hates this word. How dare God be so capricious? To call this a test doesn't exonerate him. It turns him into a sadistic schoolmaster. I suspect Dawkins feels this way because he finds it impossible that God might be wiser than he is.

Why does this matter? Well, any discerning reader approaching Genesis 22 is going to wonder, Why is God commanding child sacrifice? That's a script for Molech, not the Lord. So the question nags at us. Like a rattle in the engine, we wonder why it's there and whether something might be terminally wrong with this God we've been told to trust.

Some might say, "Well, he didn't *actually* command Abraham to kill his son." But arguing that takes some Olympic-level interpretive gymnastics. It's true: Abraham intended to kill Isaac. Moses is clear about this. So how do we untangle the knot of whether the Lord is immoral for commanding an immoral action?

That word *test* is our skeleton key. The Lord's command doubles as a one-question exam: "Abraham, do you trust me?" Now, he's taken this exam a few times before and got an F (Genesis 12, 16, 20). Of course, one party already knows everything that's about to happen. So this test isn't filling in a gap in the Lord's understanding, it's filling in a gap in Abraham's faith.

Okay, okay. I get it. I can practically feel your eyebrows furrowing. I can hear your eyeballs clanging as they roll to the back of your skull. You might think I'm the worst public defender around and that my defense for the Lord here lacks both sense and sensitivity. At the same time, you remember the answer to the question, "Will not the Judge of all the earth do right?" (18:25). So your mind is a hung jury.

If I've described you, then perhaps when the rubber meets the road, you—a bit like Abraham—actually do have doubts about God's character. Perhaps they're tiny doubts, minuscule curiosities. You know who he says he is, but your experience has piled up evidence to the contrary. Your circumstances prosecute the Lord, and sometimes, if you're honest, they make a compelling case. That's okay. We've all been there. But we do need to be careful. Even the tiniest cracks in a home's foundation need to be addressed before they expand and make the whole structure lopsided and unsafe.

No doubt, Genesis 22 tests Abraham's mettle. Look again at the request. It's as if God is sharpening his, to borrow a phrase from Dawkins, "murdering knife." "Take your son, your only son, whom you love—Isaac . . ." With every phrase, sparks fly as the blade gets sharper and sharper, as the wound in Abraham's heart gets deeper and deeper.

Since we've been taking a tour of Abraham's life, we should realize that this request applies unbelievable pressure to his weakest point, that gnawing question he's asked himself for years: "Will God really keep his promise to me?" He'd previously answered this with a "no, he won't." So he lied and committed adultery and lied some more.

But how will Abraham respond this time? Has he changed? Immediately, we realize he has: "Early the next morning Abraham got up and loaded his donkey. He took with him two of his servants and his son Isaac" (22:3).

Which brings me to my second overlooked observation.

2. Abraham expects Isaac to die, and Abraham expects Isaac to rise again. The easiest way to argue for this would be to immediately jump to Hebrews 11. But don't do that just yet. Let's see a few details here in Genesis 22 and then remind ourselves of a detail we've already covered.

Look again at Genesis 22:5. What does Abraham say to these young men who went with him before he and Isaac left for Mount Moriah?

"Stay here with the donkey while I and the boy go over there. We will worship and then we will come back to you" (22:5). Unless Abraham is deceiving his two servants, which we have no reason to believe, it's clear from this statement that he believes his son Isaac will come back with him. And it's clear from the subsequent moments—which Moses narrates detail by detail, building tension with every movement—that Abraham *also* believed he would kill his son.

Does Genesis 22:7–8 destroy this thesis? With wood strapped to his back, Isaac asks an innocent question. But for us readers, who have a wider lens than Isaac, it's haunting: "The fire and wood are here, but where is the lamb for the burnt offering?" Abraham responds somewhat enigmatically, "God himself will provide the lamb for the burnt offering, my son."

Suddenly, we're face to face with an interpretive difficulty: Is "my son" appositional or affectionate? Is Abraham saying, "My son, don't worry—God will provide a lamb," or is he saying, "God will provide a lamb—that is, my son"? I'm convinced it's the latter, though it's possible Abraham originally meant the former but, as the sand ran out of the hourglass, he slowly realized that though his heart had planned a way, the Lord had determined his steps.

So evidence is right there in Genesis 22. But let's rewind the tape. Do you remember why Sarah laughed in Genesis 18? She laughed because her menopause (18:11) meant her womb could no longer usher in life. To speak somewhat crassly, it had died.

In this book, I'm giving you a guided tour of Genesis. When we came across Genesis 12, I took us to Galatians 3. Now we need to take a quick detour to Hebrews 11 to see how later, Spirit-inspired authors understood Genesis 22.

Here's the author of Hebrews:

By faith Abraham obeyed when he was called to go out to a place that he was to receive as an inheritance. And he went out, not knowing where he was going. By faith he went to live in the land of promise, as in a foreign land, living in tents with Isaac and Jacob, heirs with him of the same promise. For he was looking forward to the city that has foundations, whose designer and builder is God. By faith Sarah herself received power to conceive, *even when she was past the age*, since she considered him faithful who had promised. Therefore from one man, *and him as good as dead*, were born descendants as many as the stars of heaven and as many as the innumerable grains of sand by the seashore.

—*Hebrews 11:8–12 ESV, italics added*

Wait a second! That's not about Abraham killing Isaac. That's about the happier seasons in Abraham's life. Quit doing eisegesis, which is just a fancy word for hermeneutical moonwalking, which is a phrase I just made up for when we start with a conclusion and then theatrically reason backward. And you're right, but this passage in Hebrews gives us vital information, which I helpfully italicized. Because our inspired color commentator keeps going:

By faith Abraham, when he was tested, offered up Isaac, and he who had received the promises was in the act of offering up his only son, of whom it was said, "Through Isaac shall your offspring be named." He considered that God was able even to raise him from the dead, from which, figuratively speaking, he did receive him back.

—*Hebrews 11:17–19 ESV*

The author of Hebrews understands what Moses is up to. He knows this was a test (11:17; cf. 22:1). But how does he also know that Abraham "considered that God was able even to raise [Isaac] from the dead"? I mean, it's not like resurrections happened in Abraham's ancient world.

Two reasons: first, because that's what happened in Genesis 22, at least figuratively (Heb. 11:19). Abraham's slaughtering knife hung ominously over Isaac's neck (Gen. 22:10). He was as good as dead. But then he heard something—not a rattle in the engine but a rustling in the thicket (22:13). God intervened. What mercy.

But there's a second and more important reason Abraham believed Isaac would be raised from the dead. It's because Abraham's life had already been defined by resurrection. After Abraham heard God's strange request, I can't help but wonder whether his whole life flashed before his eyes and he came to the right conclusion: the Lord can do anything, so I trust him.

Perhaps he remembered Sarah's laugh. Perhaps he remembered her droll response: "After I am worn out and my lord is old, will I now have this pleasure?" (18:12). Perhaps he remembered the Lord's gentle rebuke: "Is anything too hard for the LORD?" (18:14). Perhaps he looked back on his life and, for the first time, he finally saw what had always been there.

Abraham's life was a Rolodex of resurrection. From the moment God called him out of Ur to the moment he shouted his name— "Abraham!"—in Genesis 22:1, God had been demonstrating his resurrection power over and over and over again. That's why the author of Hebrews can say that Abraham was "as good as dead" (Heb. 11:12). He had no son, yet from him were born descendants "as numerous as the stars in the sky and as countless as the sand on the seashore" (Heb. 11:12; cf. Gen. 22:17). What mercy.

Abraham believed Isaac would die and rise again because Abraham himself had already figuratively died and rose again. He had a son! Is one resurrection too hard for the Lord? No, of course not. So why not another one?

When we read through Genesis 22, I hope we can see what Moses and the author of Hebrews saw, what Abraham saw—that nothing is too hard for the Lord. We see a story of a father's love for his son, a son's trust in his father, and a promised blessing being passed down from one generation to the next—until it reaches us. What mercy.

Of course, Genesis 22 also points us forward: to the death of the Father's only Son, Jesus, whom he loved. The connection points are so obvious as to feel allegorical: there's a loving father, an obedient son who's walking toward his death with his killing instrument strapped across his back, and a substitutionary ram.

But more subtle and significant than these details is Genesis 22's location: Mount Moriah. If you don't know, Mount Moriah is the location of the temple in Jerusalem (2 Chron. 3:1). The averted sacrifice of Isaac eventually became institutionalized for the people of God in later generations. As they sacrificed on the Temple Mount over and over and over again, Abraham's history became their history. Abraham's experience became their experience. They offered sacrifices and gave thanks to God for his continual over-and-over-and-over-again provision.

Jesus' death puts an end to all this. His precious blood saved his people and decimated any need for a repetitive sacrificial system. There's no need for the sacrifice of Isaac to be institutionalized for us today because the institution has crumbled—and in its place, there's Jesus. We don't need to make any sacrifices to reexperience salvation, we simply need to believe and believe and believe in Jesus' perfect sacrifice—over and over and over again, day after day after day. In doing so, we prove ourselves to be, just like Isaac, "children of Abraham" (Gal. 3:7, 13–14).

NINE

GENESIS 23:1–25:18

Why should I shrink at pain and woe?
Or feel at death dismay?
I've Canaan's goodly land in view,
And realms of endless day.

—JOSEPH BROMEHEAD, "JERUSALEM, MY HAPPY HOME"

There's no place like home.

—DOROTHY, *THE WIZARD OF OZ*

Abraham ended Genesis 22 with a sheathed knife and sharpened faith. Once led astray by his instincts of self-protection and doubt, he now walked by faith in the Lord's promises and power, so much so that he was willing to kill his only son, whom he loved, because he believed the Lord would raise him from the dead.

So what's next? At this point in the narrative, Moses is eager to conclude Abraham's story. But before he moves on, he needs to tie up a few loose ends.

To track what he's up to in these chapters, we need to track the progress of God's promises of land, seed, and blessing. More than ten chapters later, how's it going? Has he kept up his side of the bargain? Let's get a brief status update of each element of this promise, in reverse order.

Blessing. "I will bless those who bless you, and whoever curses you I will curse; and all peoples on earth will be blessed through you" (Gen. 12:3). So far, we've seen only a partial fulfillment of this promise. Negatively, we've seen Ishmael refuse to attach himself to the Lord's program, and so be cursed just like the pre-Abrahamic ancestors Cain and Ham. Positively, we've seen the Lord deal bountifully with foreign figures like Abimelek, King of Gerar (Gen. 20:14–18), and the mysterious Melchizedek (Gen. 14:17–22). So while we await a full-scale fulfillment of these promises, we've seen glimmers of its eventual success.

Blessing Status: Partially Fulfilled

Seed. "I will make you into a great nation, and I will bless you; I will make your name great, and you will be a blessing" (Gen. 12:2). You can't become a great nation without a first son. And through many dangers, toils, and snares, Abraham has indeed received the down payment on this promise: Isaac. In fact, we spent much of Genesis 12–22 anticipating the fulfillment of this promise.

Seed Status: Fulfilled

Land. "Go from your country, your people and your father's household to the land I will show you" (Gen. 12:1; restated more specifically in 15:18–21). At first, Abraham was a peripatetic patriarch (12:4–9). Then a famine redirected him to Egypt. We know what happened there: he lied, he got kicked out by a freaked-out Pharaoh, and he and his crew ended up back in the Negeb—only this time with lots of extra stuff. Oh, and Lot's stuff, too. They ultimately split up. Lot ended up near Sodom. Sadly, we know what happened there, too. Abraham, meanwhile, ended up "settling" in Canaan (13:12).

Does this mean Abraham had a Canaanite address? We need to play close attention to how Moses communicates these relocations. He wants us to know that this land was in no way, shape, or form

Abraham's. It was overrun by Canaanites and their cronies (13:7). It still belonged to Abraham's enemies, which means that Abraham had no place to call home. He had no "Live, Laugh, Love" sign above his well in Abimelek's neighborhood (21:22–33). If he had a sign, it probably said something like "Settle and Survive." As of Genesis 23, he's still a homeless sojourner, a guy renting space in occupied land.[1] Moses couldn't be clearer about this. Check out the last verse of Genesis 21: "And Abraham sojourned many days in the land of the Philistines" (21:34 ESV).

Land Status: Unfulfilled

In Genesis 22, Moses slowed down to tell a poignant story about Abraham's faith. But that pesky truth from Genesis 21:34 still hangs over the situation: Abraham has no land! And what do landless people do when one of their own dies?

This question brings us to Genesis 23.

GENESIS 23 // DEATH IN THE NEGEB

After the matriarch of the Lord's people died "in the land of Canaan" (23:2), Abraham mourns his loss. At this point, we expect the story to shuffle forward. It's quite common for deaths in Genesis to thrust the reader forward. But Moses slows down again because Sarah's death poses a unique problem: there's nowhere for Abraham to bury his wife. He has no family plot somewhere in the Negeb. He admits as much to the Hittites: "I am a sojourner and foreigner among you" (23:4 ESV). And then he makes a request.

What happens next seems so strange. Abraham and Ephron the Hittite haggle and haggle and haggle over a grave in a cave like two

---

1. When you read "homeless," don't picture someone sleeping under a bridge. Picture a Manhattanite who makes six figures but still can't afford a down payment on a Chelsea flat. Abraham has lots of resources at his disposal! But he has no land that he can call his own. He is renting someone's space and biding his time, which sounds like a Bob Dylan lyric.

couples haggling over the dinner bill. *I got it. No, I got it. Seriously, we don't mind—please let us pay.* By the end of the interaction, Abraham insists on paying four hundred shekels for "the field of Ephron in Machpelah, . . . the field with the cave that was in it and all the trees that were in the field" (23:17 ESV).

Why all the fuss about funeral finances? Why does Abraham reject the offer to bury Sarah in the choicest Hittite tomb and instead settle for the cave of Machpelah? That's like choosing a brittle pine coffin over a rich mahogany one, the Pinto over the Porsche. Oh, and why does Moses spend so much time on this? Because of Genesis 12:2. Abraham's exchange with Ephron means that he can—at last!—point to a meager sliver of Mesopotamia and say, "Mine!"

What God had promised finally had been granted. The cave of Machpelah is the first deposit of a much larger inheritance. This divinely promised and now legally purchased grave in a cave will become the temporary resting place for the first members of the Lord's family as they await resurrection into their everlasting home.[2]

Land status: Partially Fulfilled.

Now that the issue of land is settled, Moses is almost ready to shift his focus from Abraham to Isaac. But not yet. He still wants to tie up a few more loose ends. He did that in Genesis 23 with a funeral, and he does it again in Genesis 24 with a wedding.

GENESIS 24 // MY BIG, FAT, NON-CANAANITE WEDDING

When I was in high school, one of my mentors distilled the whole of his dating advice down to a single aphorism: "Don't drink, cuss, or chew—or run with girls who do."[3] I admit this counsel is more prosaic

---

2. More on that later, especially when we get near the end of the book of Genesis.
3. Rick Bordas, who's now with the Lord. I can't wait to see him again.

than Mosaic. But certain biblical characters would have fared a lot better if they'd listened to my friend's wisdom. Remember Lot's wife? She longed for the world and in doing so lost her soul. Remember Ishmael's possibly arranged marriage to a woman from Egypt? That signaled Ishmael and Hagar's rejection of God's program, their swatting away of his open hand of mercy.

Imagine reading about Ishmael's marriage as a recently freed Israelite, heels still cracked from all the desert wandering. How do you think you would have swallowed Moses' description? "[Ishmael] lived in the wilderness of Paran, and his mother took a wife for him from the land of Egypt" (21:21 ESV).

If we're reading carefully, we see that statements like these aren't Moses' vaguely celebratory additions to the Lifestyle Section of ancient Israel's newspaper. Far from it. They are, to extend the metaphor, byte-sized editorials that condemn the actions of, in this case, Ishmael and his mother. *Egypt? Why Egypt!*

So far, Moses has relied on piled-up implications when he describes these instances of unholy matrimony. Eventually, the implicit will become explicit. But we're not there yet. Instead, we're simply left with an unarticulated piece of advice that is both Mosaic and prosaic: it really matters who you marry. Which brings us to Genesis 24.

In this chapter, Moses tells the story of Abraham sending his best servant on a mission: to find a wife for Isaac. What is this nameless servant supposed to look for? Not blond hair and blue eyes but something else:

- She must not be from the Canaanites, even though that's where Abraham now lives (24:3).
- She must be from "my country and . . . my kindred" (24:4 ESV)—that is, Nahor. Though he hasn't lived there for more than one hundred years, and though it's more than five hundred miles away, that's where the servant needs to go. This preference has nothing to do with ethnic bias and everything to do with religious

belief; it has nothing to do with being ethnically intermingled but, to use a New Testament phrase, is about being "unequally yoked" (2 Cor. 6:14 KJV).

- She must be willing to come back with Abraham's servant (24:6–8). She must not act like Hagar and leave behind the Lord's people because she doesn't believe his promises. She must move her life and plant roots in the promised land.

That's Abraham's criteria, and we should notice how he roots it all in God's prior promises (24:7).

But wait a minute, this is a backward courtship strategy. It's less promising than speed dating, more volatile than an ancient Near Eastern version of *The Bachelor*. When the servant arrives at his destination, he makes the unlikely situation even more dire by adding yet another, ad hoc expectation: Isaac's prospective wife must show hospitality to his thirsty camels (24:12–14).

As readers, we're supposed to catch the absurd impracticality of all this. But the Lord loves to subvert our expectations. If we're paying attention, it's clear the Lord is orchestrating this "love story." He honors the servant's request and, "before [the servant has] finished speaking," Rebekah shows up and immediately checks nearly every box. First, she's from the right family and the right place; she's Abraham's grandniece (24:15). Second, she's generous and hospitable (24:17–20). She cares for the servant and his camels.

The servant can't quite believe his fortune. He's dumbstruck, like Bugs Bunny with hearts in his eyes (24:21). Could it be, he wonders, that she's the one? Pretty quickly, we see the answer is yes. The servant can't help but give praise to God for his "kindness and faithfulness" to Abraham (24:27).

That phrase is important. It's repeated throughout the chapter (24:12, 14, 27, 49) because it underscores that all of this is happening because the Lord is remaining faithful to his promise to Abraham. Even as the main characters change—Abraham gives way to Isaac, Sarah to

Rebekah—Moses' message remains the same. The Lord is invested in Isaac's finding a suitable wife because he's made promises about Isaac's son and Isaac's sons' sons and their sons after them. He's promised to turn this fledgling family into a blessed nation. I'll say it again: it really matters who you marry.

Then Rebekah's brother Laban shows up. How will he respond to his lovestruck sister? At first, he comes across as hospitable and gregarious. He embraces Abraham's servant and ushers him into his home, offering him something to eat (24:29–33).

Over the next sixteen verses (24:34–49), Moses places his prior narration onto the lips of Abraham's servant. In his speech to Laban, we learn a few new tidbits—how Abraham encouraged his fearful servant (24:40), where the gold ring went (24:47)—but not much. The goal of the speech is to get Rebekah's family to underwrite the relationship, to agree that it's all from the Lord.

Laban and Bethuel—Rebekah's brother and father—agree and then appear to send their sister and daughter on her way (24:50–51). Abraham's servant responds by eliminating any need for Isaac and Rebekah to visit Target for their wedding registry (24:53).

And then, quite literally overnight, what started as fast and frictionless becomes slow and stumbling. Moses doesn't explain why Laban suddenly seems so eager to gum up their engagement. But he's given us a few clues. Notice what catches Laban's eye in 24:30: "As soon as he had seen the nose ring, and the bracelets on his sister's arms . . ." Notice also how Moses prefaces Laban's demand for a delay: "The servant brought out gold and silver jewelry and articles of clothing and gave them to Rebekah; he also gave costly gifts to her brother and to her mother" (24:53).

In Genesis 24, we see two members of the same family displaying generous hospitality for opposite reasons. It seems Laban gives of himself to receive more for himself. That explains the delay—perhaps he sees an opportunity to squeeze more out of Abraham's servant. In doing so, he shows the man not steadfast love but proof of his own selfishness. He rejects the Lord even as he acknowledges his sovereignty over a situation he seeks to manipulate for his own gain.[4]

Rebekah, it seems, is the opposite. She gives of herself to receive nothing at all. Notice what catches her eye in 24:17: a man and a few camels in need. Notice also that she did all this "quickly" and of her own volition (24:18–20). From beginning to end, she shows this servant both steadfast love and proof of her selflessness. Like her great-uncle before her, she embraces and responds to the Lord's life-altering invitation with "I will go" (24:58).

Hopefully, you can see at least one lesson from this chapter quite clearly: Laban's parade of piety is just that—a parade, nothing more than a momentary celebration designed to elicit a positive response from his audience. Rebekah's piety, on the other hand, isn't performative. It's from the heart.

After this back and forth, Rebekah's family does finally "bless" her marriage (24:60) with words that recall the Lord's promises to Abraham in Genesis 22:15–18. This connection highlights Rebekah's role in proving the Lord's kindness and faithfulness by providing a next generation for his promised people. To use Laban's phrase, which he may not have meant himself, all of this has "come from the LORD" (24:50 ESV).

Okay, so what's the point of all this?

Again, Moses is tidying up loose ends as he shifts from the first generation to the second. Sarah has died; Rebekah has proven herself to be worthy of taking the mantle as Israel's matriarch. The story can now move on. The Lord's promises didn't expire with the expiration of Abraham and Sarah. They carry on through sobering funerals, dramatic weddings, and—as we're about to see—the birth of oppositional twins.[5]

---

4. This won't be the last time we see Laban play this card.

5. In episode 8 of *Bible Talk*, Sam vociferously suggests that the story of Rebekah is a preview of the exodus. "Moses sees correspondences between what happens in the lives of the patriarchs and the events that he and Israel went through in the exodus. So he crafts these stories in such a way to bring these parallels out . . . to encourage the people of Israel . . . to

GENESIS 25:1-18 // EAST OF BEER-LAHAI-ROI

We've seen before that genealogies are Moses' version of a literary time-travel device, a way of pressing fast-forward. That's most of Genesis 25, which features the death of the Bible's main human character: Abraham. Here's how Moses writes the patriarch's obituary:

> These are the days of the years of Abraham's life, 175 years. Abraham breathed his last and died in a good old age, an old man and full of years, and was gathered to his people. Isaac and Ishmael his sons buried him in the cave of Machpelah, in the field of Ephron the son of Zohar the Hittite, east of Mamre, the field that Abraham purchased from the Hittites. There Abraham was buried, with Sarah his wife. After the death of Abraham, God blessed Isaac his son. And Isaac settled at Beer-lahai-roi.
>
> —*Genesis 25:7–11 ESV*

A few details stand out. First, it's striking that both Isaac and Ishmael bury their father (25:9). Though we know next to nothing about Ishmael's relationship with his family after he left with Hagar to marry an Egyptian, it's simultaneously heartwarming and harrowing that he shows up for his father's funeral. It's heartwarming because we now know Genesis 21 doesn't end in Ishmael's total alienation from

---

trust God, to trust his ways, that he's going to deliver on the exodus program in the conquest just as he did for the patriarchs."

Here's his argument: Rebekah is dwelling outside the land of promise; Abraham sends a servant, who reminds us of Moses (Deut. 34:5); that servant is also reluctant at first, like Moses; the angel of the Lord paves the way for both servants (Gen. 24:7, 40; Ex. 23:20); Laban hesitates like Pharaoh; and then at the end the servant secures a bride for Isaac. He sums up Genesis 24 as follows: "There's a general pattern that seems to mirror this angel of the Lord who leads a servant that's going to take someone from a foreign land and bring them back into the promised land."

PS: When you get to Genesis 26 and 28, see if you recognize any similar exodus-adjacent patterns.

PPS: Sam definitely does.

his family. It's harrowing because in Ishmael we see an example of the difficult-to-stomach truth that proximity to God's blessings doesn't make us recipients of God's blessings. More on Ishmael in a second.

Second, that legally purchased grave in a cave shows up again, highlighting once more how vital it was for Abraham to legally purchase in full that land from Ephron the Hittite.

Third and finally, the Lord himself blesses Isaac after Abraham's death and in doing so passes the baton from one generation to the next. Moses has already described Isaac's pride of place at the beginning of this chapter. Though the sons of Keturah receive gifts (25:6) from Abraham, Isaac receives everything his father had (25:5). They inherit neither the blessing nor the land, hence their relocation to the east country (25:6).

So that's what happened to Abraham's other sons. But what about Ishmael? Moses has one more loose end to tie up, and so he gives us Ishmael's genealogy (25:12–18), which yet again shows that the Lord always keeps his promises. We've already seen how his promises to Ishmael are different from his promises to Isaac. Both will become great nations. Isaac will sire kings, yet Ishmael will sire mere princes. Both will be blessed, yet God establishes his covenant only with Isaac. Ishmael's genealogy makes good on God's promise as Moses introduces us to "twelve princes according to their tribes" (25:16 ESV).

We need to remember that these genealogical narrations are rarely neutral. That's why Moses can't help but remind us where these princes ("tribal rulers" NIV) end up: near Egypt in the direction of Ashur (25:18). This branch of the family tree eventually yields the bitter fruit of Israel's most stubborn, most hostile enemies.[6]

So as we conclude the story of Abraham and turn the page to his lineage, let's take stock of where we are. Moses has detailed the half-dozen sons of Abraham's concubine and the dozen royal sons of

---

6. Ashur is the home of the people who become Assyrians. Interestingly, Isaiah 10:15 describes Assyria as a God-wielded axe that strikes at the root of Israel.

Abraham's mistress. Father Abraham had many sons; many sons had father Abraham. But the son of promise? His line is a fledgling, solitary sprout amid a field marked by others' obvious fruitfulness.

Imagine for a second that you don't know the ending of the story. You might come to Genesis 25:18 with a few questions. "Hang on a second. Will the Lord's promise really extend through Isaac, the so-called miracle only-child whose birth made his parents laugh? Why wouldn't he choose the royal sons of the outdoorsy bow expert?"

But if we're asking questions like these—whether about these early chapters of Genesis or the unfolding chapters of our own lives—then it's clear that we need to either remember or learn for the first time what our main character Abraham finally learned.

The Lord can do anything, and it's our job to trust him.

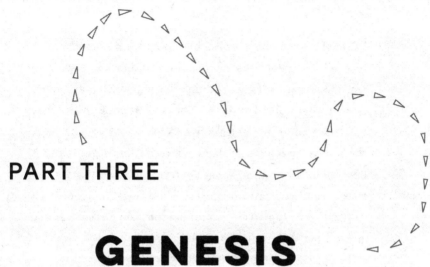

PART THREE

GENESIS
25:19-36:42

I came here tonight, and I didn't know what to expect. I've seen a lot of people hating me, and I didn't know what to feel about that. So I guess I didn't like you much none either. During this fight, I've seen a lot of changing, in the way youse felt about me and the way I felt about you. In here, there were two guys killing each other, but I guess that's better than 20 million. What I'm trying to say is that if I can change, and you can change, everybody can change!

[raucous applause, including from the Soviets, as the entire Cold War comes to an end]

—ROCKY BALBOA, *ROCKY IV*

The least degree of grace is an everlasting possession. It comes down from heaven. It is precious in our Lord's eyes. It shall never be overthrown. . . . A spark is better than utter darkness, and little faith better than no faith at all.

—J. C. RYLE, *EXPOSITORY THOUGHTS ON MATTHEW*[1]

---

1. Here, he's commenting on Matthew 12:14–21. Thanks to Nick Roark for alerting me to this quote.

TEN

GENESIS 25:19-28:9

The sins of the father are the sins of the son.
Crawl before you walk, boy, walk before you run.

–TIM MCGRAW, "WALK LIKE A MAN"

This year I'm told the team did well because one pitcher had
a fine curveball. I understand that a curveball is thrown with
a deliberate attempt to deceive. Surely this is not an ability
we should want to foster at Harvard.

–CHARLES ELIOT, PRESIDENT OF HARVARD UNIVERSITY, 1884[1]

In Genesis 24, Moses presents the microwaved matrimony of Isaac
and Rebekah. In Genesis 25:19–26:35, he presents Isaac's life as a
microwaved microcosm of Abraham's, an anthology of a son reliving
his father's greatest hits and repeating his greatest mistakes. As Moses
speeds through Isaac to get to Jacob, he wants us to see that the sins

---

1. There's some doubt about the provenance of this delectable quote. It could have been
made by his less famous cousin Charles Eliot Norton, who was a professor of art history at
Harvard the same time his cousin served as president.

and the struggles of the father are sometimes the sins and struggles of the son.

GENESIS 25:19-26 // ANOTHER TALE OF ANOTHER SET OF SONS

Right away, the similarities between the two generations are obvious. Just like Sarah, Rebekah is barren (25:21). Just like he did for Sarah, the Lord opens Rebekah's womb (25:21). And just like we saw in the previous generation, at the heart of this family will be a conflict between two brothers that we hear about through a surprising prebirth prophecy. Yet again the son of promise will be the second son; yet again "the older will serve the younger" (25:23; cf. 16:11–12).

Of course, some details differ: The Lord doesn't require Isaac and Rebekah to wait as long as Abraham and Sarah, though they still wait two decades (25:26). This time, the brothers at odds are twins, not half siblings born fifteen years apart to a pair of women who hate each other.[2] Nonetheless, the arithmetic of the situation is the same: for the Lord's promises to Abraham to advance, he must miraculously intervene.

By making these connections, Moses gives us a streamlined way to understand this new cast of characters. Isaac and Rebekah are like Abraham and Sarah, but without the concubine. Esau is like Ishmael,[3] a mighty hunter (25:27; cf. 21:20) who's cold toward the Lord and spurred on by shortsighted passions—fatigue, hunger, fury. Jacob is like Isaac and Abraham before him, a heel-grabbing homebody who struggles to trust the Lord more than his own wit and wisdom. Moses'

---

2. This distinction is vital to understanding how the apostle Paul unpacks these chapters in Romans 9. He finds the levelest playing field imaginable—brothers born at the same time, to the same mother, who share even the same moment of conception—in order to make the point that salvation depends wholly on God's mercy and nothing else. There's nothing intrinsically in us for which we can boast.

3. He's also a hunter like Nimrod (10:9) and, incidentally, a nimrod like Nimrod.

intro to this third generation encourages us to ask important questions: Is Esau's resemblance to Ishmael skin-deep, or does it run to the heart? Will Esau also reject the Lord's promises? We also wonder about Jacob. Will he follow in his grandfather's footsteps, resisting the Lord's program until he finally trusts him?

Keep these questions in mind as you read this chapter.

GENESIS 25:27-34 // AN UNFORTUNATE TRIP TO THE GROCERY STORE

If you're like me, you grew up thinking this story doubles as a warning about going to the grocery store hungry, because when you're hungry you do stupid stuff like buy eccentrically flavored Oreos and sell your birthright to your deceitful brother. It's a story about the dunderheaded and dangerous consequences of uncontrolled appetites. There are, I suppose, worse summaries of biblical stories, but that more or less misses the point. Esau's problem isn't that he cares too much about food but that he cares too little about his family.

Look again at this brief episode's addendum: "So Esau despised his birthright" (25:34). In this sentence, Moses tells us what he's just shown us. Esau didn't care about inheriting his father's estate. He didn't care about his firstborn right as head of the household.[4] Why? Perhaps he didn't think much of what the Lord had promised to do through Abraham. Perhaps he'd grown up knowing the upside-down prophecy about how he'd serve his brother and it embittered him, even though he was his father's preferred son. We don't know the why, but we know the what: this birthright meant nothing to him, so he sold it for a bowl of soup.[5]

---

4. See Deut. 21:17 for the way this worked. In short, the oldest son normally gets a double portion.

5. Was Esau really about to die? No, I don't think so. He was exaggerating or, as my kids say, "being dramatic." We use exaggeration all the time in our speech, especially with friends and family. Or in sentences that begin with "we use exaggeration all the time." Here's a more

Does this mean Esau will end up like Ishmael? Will he abandon his family altogether? We don't have a definitive answer, but the early returns aren't looking good.

GENESIS 26:1-33 // "OH, YOU LOOK JUST LIKE YOUR DAD!"

Here's the headline of Genesis 26: Isaac is just like his dad. He's both blessed and boneheaded. In fact, Isaac's relocation in Genesis 26 is so similar to his father's in Genesis 12 that Moses flags it for us (26:1). You'll remember how Abraham's famine-fueled trip to Egypt turned out (12:10–20)—pretty bad, except for all the riches. The Lord wants Isaac to avoid this fate, so he shows up and basically tells Isaac, "Don't be an idiot and go to Egypt like your dad. Stay here in Gerar." Then he proceeds to shower Isaac with the same promises he made to Abraham—promises about land, seed, and blessing, the whole covenant kit and caboodle (26:2–5).

Isaac stays put, and for a brief moment we imagine that he is less like his dad than we thought. But as the old saying goes, you can keep a man out of Egypt, but you can't keep the "lying to a king about his wife being his sister" out of a man. Isaac stays in the right place, but he does the wrong thing. He tells the same lie ("She's my sister!") to the same man (Abimelek) for the same self-serving reasons (fear of imminent death), which provokes the same response ("What have you done to us?") and the same realization for us as readers (the Lord's blessings will march on despite the sins of these people).

The rest of Genesis 26 is more of the same. Moses compresses Isaac's life into a SparkNotes version of Abraham's:

---

fascinating question to ask: Did Esau know about the prophecy? I'd offer a tentative no, but he certainly knew his father loved him and his mother loved his brother; Moses tells us as much (25:28). I suspect he always wondered why, but his father didn't have the heart to tell him.

- He gets rich. Compare 26:12–15 with 12:16 and 13:2.
- There's drama over some wells between Isaac, Abimelek, and Abimelek's goons. Compare 26:17–25 and 21:25–26.
- Isaac, Abimelek, and Abimelek's goons patch it up, shake hands, and share a meal. Compare 26:26–33 and 21:22–23.[6]

With that, Moses is ready to move on to the next generation. And he begins with a heartbreaking story.

GENESIS 26:34-28:9 // A FIVE-SENSES BETRAYAL + A FORK IN THE ROAD

Do you remember my mentor's dating wisdom? We already saw how Ishmael ignored it when he married the nameless Egyptian (21:21). Well, so does Esau. Twice. He marries Judith, which is a mistake because she's a Hittite. Then he marries Basemath, which is a mistake because she's also a Hittite, and because he's already married, and probably because her name was Basemath.[7] Moses doesn't mince any words about how Esau's polyamory alienates him from his family. These wives, he tells us, are a source of grief (26:35); they disgust Rebekah (27:46) and seem to animate her destructive plan in the story that follows.

Before we run through any details, let me quickly address two questions that will frame how we understand what's to come.

First, how do we distinguish between the birthright Esau already sold and the blessing Isaac now wants to give him? They're clearly not the same things (Gen. 27:36). Here's the easiest way I know how to answer this question: the difference between a birthright and

---

6. In both cases, this buddy-buddy conversation happens at Beersheba, which is a bit odd because you would think Isaac and Abimelek wouldn't need to do the same thing at the same place a generation later. You'd think the agreement would have survived from Abraham to Isaac. But clearly it didn't.

7. My apologies to any book-reading Basemaths out there.

a blessing is similar to the difference between a square and a rectangle. All birthrights are blessings, but not every blessing is tied to a birthright. Usually, the oldest son receives both the birthright and the greatest blessing, but in Genesis that pattern is flipped more than it's followed.[8] Generally speaking, birthrights pertain to the father's present-day property being passed down—think cattle, clothes, that kind of stuff—while blessings pertain to a son's future trajectory—think of Noah's enigmatic antiblessings in 9:24–27.[9]

A second question is more difficult to answer: Was Isaac wrong to want to give this blessing to Esau? The answer to that is probably. I'll explain why in a moment.

There are three people in this story other than Esau. We should assume both Rebekah and Isaac know the Lord's prophecy in Genesis 25:23.[10] We should also reasonably assume that Jacob knows, because he and his mom are as thick as thieves. Let's break down what happens character by character.

- *Isaac.* Isaac says he's about to die.[11] And then he proposes a stubborn plan: he wants to bless Esau, not Jacob. Of course, that's the opposite of what the Lord promised. Why does Isaac want to resist the Lord? Moses doesn't tell us, except for the detail that Isaac prefers Esau for superficial reasons (25:28).
- *Rebekah.* When Rebekah overhears her husband's stubborn plan to bless the unblessed son, she devises—with frightening speed—a

---

8. For example: Isaac over Ishmael, Jacob over Esau, Joseph and Judah over their brothers, and Ephraim over Manasseh.

9. Perhaps the clearest example of this will come at the end of Genesis when Jacob blesses his twelve sons (49:1–27).

10. Moses doesn't tell us explicitly that Rebekah tells Isaac about the prophecy. But that sentence "she went to inquire of the LORD" in 25:22 can be understood as Rebekah's looking for a prophet via her husband. This is the case Jim makes in the relevant episode of *Bible Talk*. If this is the case, then the Lord's response in the next verse would have been to both of them. Of course, she also could have just told him later on. It's unclear whether Jacob knows, though perhaps he's fearful of losing his future blessing if he gets caught trying to deceive his father. (See 27:12.)

11. Like Esau, he's wrong. He somehow stays alive until Genesis 35, like how Clint Eastwood is somehow still directing movies.

stubborn plan of her own. Why does Rebekah want to take this situation into her own hands? Again, Moses doesn't tell us, but he has given relevant details: Rebekah prefers Jacob (25:28) and is disgusted by Esau's wives (27:46). It's tempting to defend Rebekah here: she's just preventing her husband from doing something he shouldn't do! But we shouldn't excuse her taking advantage of her husband's age and appetite. In fact, Rebekah's plan for her son should remind us of Sarai's plan for her husband in Genesis 16. Why? Because it relies on sinful human behavior to manufacture divine fulfillment. As Sarai and Rebekah stared down the barrel of barrenness and blindness, respectively, they wondered whether the Lord had been outfoxed by human frailty. So they got to work—and both times the consequences split these families in two.

- *Jacob.* I kind of feel bad for Jacob. After all, this isn't his idea, and he does at least try to resist his mother. But like an ice cube on a summer sidewalk, he melts. He obeys her voice and agrees to pry from his father's hand what the Lord had already promised him. Delayed disobedience is still, well, disobedience.

- *Esau.* I really feel bad for Esau. He's the main victim here—of his father's delusion, his mother's disdain, his brother's deception. He doesn't deserve what happens to him, and our hearts should break with his as he cries out to his empty-handed father. And yet we should ask why Moses frames this unholy heist with comments about Esau's unholy marriages (26:34–35; 27:46). Perhaps it's because he wants us to remember that this son of Isaac would rather attach himself to two Hittite women than to the Lord.

So that's the why, as best as we can tell.

Now let's talk about the what of Isaac blessing Jacob Whom He Thinks Is Esau (27:27–29). This isn't a generic Hallmark card: "I am so blessed to have you as a son." It's not one of those jokey cards that's emblazoned with an embarrassing dad-joke: "Blessings to you, Esau, my 'soup-er' son." No, these blessings are specific. Better yet, they're Abrahamic, especially the last part. Isaac blends what the Lord told his father in Genesis 12 and what the Lord told him in Genesis 25 and then serves it up.

But hang on! He shouldn't be doing this. We should see this not as ignorance but as obstinance. Isaac's doing what he wants. He wants to bless his preferred son. And he doesn't realize his opposition to the Lord is achieving the opposite effect until it's too late.

Which brings us to the climax of the story. Look again at the details. Each one breaks your heart. Esau finally shows up right after Jacob leaves (27:30). He's got soup in his hand and a smile on his face (27:31). He coaxes his father to sit up so he can fill his belly before giving his blessing (27:31). It's an intimate moment.

And then comes a question a father should never have to ask his son: "Who are you?" (27:32) And when he hears Esau's answer—with every phrase more specific than the last—the knife that Isaac avoided on Mount Moriah gets plunged into his heart.

I am your son . . . Your firstborn . . . Esau . . .

When Isaac realizes what he's done and who he's blessed, Moses tells us, Isaac "trembled violently" (27:33).

You might be tempted to ask Isaac why he doesn't just take it back. Why doesn't he just press Control-Z and reverse his mistaken blessing as an administrative error?

He doesn't because he doesn't want to. He doesn't because he's finally learned what his father learned years before: the Lord's purposes always prevail, even when—or perhaps especially when—our sin tries to get in the way. When someone "trembles violently" in the Old Testament, it's because they've encountered the presence of the Lord.[12] That's what happens here.

Once Isaac realizes he's been fooled by trusting in everything else

---

12. That word for "trembled violently" shows up only a few times: 1 Sam. 14:15; Jer. 30:5; and Dan. 10:7.

but the Lord, once he realizes that all five of his senses have outfoxed him,[13] he sobers up enough to tell his favored son the difficult truth (27:35–40).[14]

The first chunk of Genesis 28 cements the brothers' separation. Like his father before him (24:3), Jacob receives his matrimonial marching orders: don't marry a Canaanite. We'll see how that gets resolved in the next chapter. And also like his father before him, he receives Abraham's blessing (28:4) and all its accompanying benefits. They're all there: land, seed, and blessing.

These gifts fuel Esau's fury. Though he once lived for his father's pleasure, though he once begged for his blessing and cried out for his affirmation, now he wants nothing to do with them. His realization in Genesis 28:8 offers a fork in the road. But instead of turning back, he marches on. Esau marries still more foreign women. In fact, he salts the wound by marrying, of all people, *Ishmael's daughter* (Gen. 28:9). This certainly compounds his father's displeasure and finally severs for good any knot that tied him to his family.

From this point on, Esau is committed to vengeance, Jacob is on the run, and Rebekah is full of disgust. Isaac, meanwhile, is still half blind. All he can see is wreckage: brother against brother, wife against husband, father and mother against son. All we can see is yet another fractured family, yet another branch of the tree that has been poisoned by a refusal to trust the Lord.

---

13. Okay, here's a list:
   - Sight (27:1ff.)
   - Hearing (27:19, 22). Admittedly, Isaac is suspicious of the voice, but the suspicion fades.
   - Smell (27:27)
   - Taste (27:25)
   - Touch (27:21–23)

14. Notice how Esau receives no land, no blessing, and no enduring seed. Instead, it appears his life will be fraught with friction and heartache.

ELEVEN

GENESIS 28:10-31:55

Yeah she'll take her time but I don't mind
Waitin' on a woman.

—BRAD PAISLEY, "WAITIN' ON A WOMAN"

We burn with a desire to settle ourselves, but mistake the
way, and build castles in the air, which vanish like bubbles
of soap in water.

—STEPHEN CHARNOCK, 1628-80

From now until Genesis 36, Jacob is the main character of this story. So let's take a quick inventory of what Moses has told us about him: he's an opportunist, a trickster, a scoundrel, and a homebody. He's tossed to and fro by the whims of his mother. Freudians would have a field day. Am I missing anything?

And yet the Lord's blessing now sits atop his seemingly unfit shoulders. The hope of humanity—the seed of the woman who would inherit the Lord's promises of land and blessing, the one whose seed would one day crush the head of the serpent—yeah, all *that* now sits atop the shoulders of a shyster and a momma's boy.

Gulp.

But we shouldn't be surprised. This third link in the chain of promise—from Abraham to Isaac to Jacob—tells the same story: God is sovereign in salvation and in judgment. This reality in no way impugns his character or undermines our responsibility.

I've mentioned this already in a footnote but it's worth reiterating. What I just said is the apostle Paul's deduction from the story of Jacob and Esau: before these twin baby boys had done anything good or evil—before Jacob lied and cosplayed as his hairy brother, before Esau chose food over faith, before any of that—the Lord chose Jacob for salvation. Why? Not because Jacob's deeds deserved salvation but so that the Lord's own purpose in election might stand (Rom. 9:11). After reading that, if your teeth clench and your eyebrows mush together and you wonder—silently, because it would seem imprudent to say stuff like this out loud—"Well, this all seems sort of unfair," then I would respond, "Well done!" That's proof you're tracking with the Bible's logic. Keep reading Romans 9, especially verses 14–29, to see how the Lord answers that objection.[1]

The Lord's salvation isn't like getting into Harvard or buying a used car. It doesn't matter who your daddy is and you can't qualify with good credit. No, to use Paul's lingo, the children of promise—or, to use Moses' lingo, the "seed of the woman"; or, to use normal people's lingo, "Christians"—lay claim to their salvation not by pointing to anything in themselves but by pointing to everything in the Lord. His inexhaustible mercy far exceeds our decent morality. He saves us.

Part of the conceit of this book is to grab you by the scruff of your collar and help you understand that you can understand Genesis. But don't get it twisted: just because you understand Genesis doesn't mean you fully understand the Lord of Genesis. He is transcendent. He is

---

1. Buckle up. Those are what I like to call worldview-altering verses.

unlike us. His mercy and judgment are as attractive as they are confounding. His communication is clear, but it is never comprehensive. It cannot be. He is the potter, and we are the clay.

So far, Jacob doesn't seem to get this. He might be happy to admit he's clay, but he really prefers to mold his circumstances to his liking. Because of this, he's been unmoved by the Lord's mercy. In fact, Jacob and the Lord don't really seem to have any kind of relationship. The Lord has talked *about* Jacob but never *to* him. That's all about to change.

GENESIS 28:10-22 // A STAIRWAY TO HEAVEN ON THE WAY TO HARRAN

When Jacob sets out to find a wife, he heads to Harran. Harran is named after Haran—Abraham's brother, Lot's father. It's where Jacob's extended family lives. Apparently they never left their hometown. When Jacob gets there, he's supposed to find his uncle Laban and marry one of his daughters (27:43; 28:2).

But in the middle of his journey, Jacob is interrupted by a dream. Moses sets the scene for us in a way that reminds us of Genesis 15.[2] You'll remember how in that chapter the Lord divinely interrupted Abraham with a bizarre covenant ceremony. What we get here is less weird, but still unusual. In Genesis 15, the Lord—as a smoking firepot and a flaming torch—walks a bloody road that unnervingly signifies his unswerving commitment to Jacob's sleeping grandfather. In Genesis 28, the Lord stands at the top of an angelic elevator, a stairway to heaven, and communicates his unswerving commitment to Abraham's sleeping grandson. Jacob has just heard these promises from his father, but now he hears them from the Lord.

---

2. In both scenes, the sun is setting and the main character is asleep. (Compare 15:12 and 28:11.) Also in both scenes, the Lord identifies himself: "I am the Lord" (15:7; 28:13).

This is the first interaction between Jacob and the Lord, and what follows in 28:13–15 is essentially a restatement of Abraham's greatest hits from Genesis 12–15. From descendants like the dust (13:16) to the direction of the land (13:14) to the declaration "I am the LORD" (15:7) to the promise to bless the peoples of the earth (12:3), we've heard all this before. Moses repeats the content and context of Abraham's blessing in order to fulfill in real time what had been prophesied at birth: Jacob is the son of promise.

How does Jacob respond (28:16–22)? At first, he remarks on the Lord's surprising presence and sets up a pillar of remembrance. So far, so good. But then, well, he seems to slip back into old habits. Never one to miss out on the best side of a deal, he makes his confidence in the Lord conditional.

We've already seen what happens when men and women hold the Lord hostage (Abraham and Hagar). We've also seen what happens when humankind tries to build its own ladder into heaven (Tower of Babel).[3] In both cases, the results are disastrous. At this point in

---

3. It's appropriate to consider this moment as a reverse Tower of Babel. It's likely that both the tower and the ladder are ancient Near Eastern ziggurats that functioned as "gateways to the gods." The terms for tower and ladder aren't obviously connected in our modern minds, but they are. Back then, a tower looked like a pyramidal structure and a ladder looked more like a stairway than a step stool.

In Genesis 11, humankind tried to claw its way up to heaven's throne room. They failed; the Lord laughed; chaos ensued. Bad execution, even worse motivation (to "make a name for ourselves"), but in theory, a good idea. Here's a quote from Sam in our conversation about this passage: "How is God going to make an access point between heaven and earth? Through this chosen seed and fulfilling his promises to this family."

That might seem like a vexing overstatement until you get to John's gospel. Jesus confronts Nazareth-hating Nathanael with a clear demonstration of his deity. Nathanael then genuflects and immediately sees Jesus as the Messiah. Here's how Jesus responds: "You believe because I told you I saw you under the fig tree. You will see greater things than that. . . . Very truly I tell you, you will see '*heaven open, and the angels of God ascending and descending on*' the Son of Man" (John 1:50–51; compare the italicized text with Gen. 28:12). Jesus tells him, "You ain't seen nothing yet."

If that was true even for Nathanael, then it was certainly true for Jacob. Jesus couldn't be clearer that he's the fulfillment of Jacob's staircase; he's the access point between heaven and earth. In Genesis 28, we get a hint of what becomes clear as day by John 1: the only way for us to go up is for the Lord to come down—not in mockery but in mercy. Jesus is the true temple, Jacob's ladder/stairway the Lord's answer to Babel.

Much of this is from Sam in *Bible Talk*, episode 9.

Genesis 28, the Lord has appeared to Jacob and mercifully made it clear that he has an important role to play in establishing the Lord's program on the earth. Unfortunately, he still has a lot to learn.

GENESIS 29:1-15 // JACOB FALLS IN LOVE, LABAN SETS THE HOOK

Jacob restarts his journey and arrives at what Moses calls "the land of the eastern peoples" (29:1). He's now east of Canaan and outside the promised land. After some chitchat with some shepherds at the local watering hole (29:2–5), we know he's in the right place: Harran.

Remember, he's on the hunt for a wife. We know this. Moses knows we know this, and so he introduces us to Laban's daughter Rachel. Immediately smitten with her, Jacob gets possessed by a kind of superhuman strength. This whole episode is supposed to be funny and endearing. Like Isaac's servant, Jacob is Bugs Bunny with hearts in his eyes. Moses isn't so obvious. He lets us do the matchmaking math: the stone over the well is large (29:2) and usually takes the strength of many men to move (29:3). But when Rachel shows up, Jacob manages to roll the stone away all by himself (29:10).[4] If you've ever been to high school—or middle school, for that matter!—then you should be able to recreate this scene in your mind rather easily.

So Jacob's in love. He kisses Rachel and begins to weep. *At last*, he thinks, *my journey to find a wife has ended!* Once he tells Rachel he's from the right family, she runs home to tell her father (29:9–12), who embraces his soon-to-be son-in-law with language that recalls the first Adam and Eve in Eden: "You are my own flesh and blood" (29:14). Surely we're about to have another wedding, right?

But hang on. We've met this guy Laban before. We've seen how

---

4. And did you catch the connection? Just as Jacob "rolled the stone away" all by himself, so the angels—three days after Jesus' death—rolled the stone . . . I'm kidding. This was a test. Some verbal connections lead to nothing but memorably stated malarkey.

his "hospitality" hides his true heart. Do you remember how Moses introduced Laban back in Genesis 24? Laban puts on a parade of piety in order to squeeze more and more out of Abraham's servant. So far, Moses has depicted Uncle Laban and Nephew Jacob as two similar characters, two self-centered deceivers. So what happens when these selfish tricksters meet? You won't be surprised at the answer.

It takes a month, but Laban eventually sets the hook: "Hang on, I know we're flesh and blood. But *surely* you don't think you'll just get her for free?" Laban seizes on his nephew's love for his daughter and, true to form, sets out to squeeze everything he can for himself.

GENESIS 29:16–30 // WAITIN' ON A WOMAN

The details of how Laban's trick comes to light are tawdry and straight-forward: at the last moment, Laban switches out beloved and beautiful Rachel for weak and overlooked Leah. Jacob recoils at his discovery. I love how Moses connects Jacob's disbelief to two previous situations in which someone has been duped. Did you catch it? Both Pharaoh and Abimelek said the same thing: "What is this you have done to me?" (12:18; 26:10; 29:25). Moses records the same words on purpose. The deceiver has become the deceived and, in the process, the seed of the woman (Jacob) has fallen prey to a scheme of the seed of the serpent (Laban). The fact that this scheme is so similar to the one Jacob's father and grandfather once employed only deepens the irony and extends the comeuppance. The Lord has been waiting to unleash this stroke of poetic justice for a few generations.[5]

By the end of Jacob's second set of seven years' service to Laban (29:30), Jacob's family is in a similar place to Abraham's, but for different reasons. Like his grandfather, Jacob is connected to two

---

5. All together now: Moses is a masterful storyteller.

women—one he loves, one he endures. We've seen how this plays out, and we've seen how spousal rivalries trickle down to sibling rivalries. From Ishmael and Isaac to Jacob and Esau, the pattern has been unbroken: when a marriage is broken, a family falls apart.[6]

GENESIS 29:31-30:24 // AN OUTRAGEOUS ORIGIN STORY PUNCTUATED BY PATHETIC PREGNANCIES

This passage tells the messy origin story of the twelve tribes of Israel. Moses starts with Leah's pathetic pregnancies.[7] Rachel, meanwhile, is barren and jealous. Moses depicts these sisters as polar opposites: Leah lacks Jacob's love and yet gives him sons; Rachel enjoys Jacob's love yet lacks the ability to give him a single son. Eventually, Leah learns that the Lord is sovereign and good and therefore worthy of her praise despite difficult circumstances (29:35). If you want to chart Leah's growth, pay attention to her kids' names. At first, she is fixated on what she lacks: a husband's love (29:32–34). But by the time Judah is born, she's focused on the Lord.

What about Rachel? Well, she's got a ways to go: "Give me children, or I'll die!" (30:1). Jacob seems to understand his relative powerlessness in this (30:2). He recognizes that the Lord opens and shuts the womb. Rachel doesn't seem to care, so she proposes a plan more pathetic than Leah's baby-naming tradition: "Here, sleep with my servant" (30:3).

Jacob obviously never read Genesis 16. But he grew up surrounded by its consequences. That's why he rarely sees his uncle Ishmael. So he must know this is a terrible idea. But he doesn't seem to care.

What happens in Genesis 30:4–13 is bizarre: it's essentially a

---

6. You could argue that this pattern began with Cain and Abel, extended to Noah's sons (though we know next to nothing about Noah's nameless wife), and even branched out to Lot's daughters.

7. I mean pathetic like Merriam-Webster means pathetic: inspiring pity and sadness.

strife-fueled baby fest in which Rachel and Leah try to one-up each other by urging their husband to sleep with other women. The names Rachel gives her servant Bilhah's kids—"God has vindicated me" and "I'm victorious over my sister"—reveal a heart poisoned by envy and self-centeredness. We're supposed to read this and feel sorry for Rachel. It's a mess. And it gets worse when Leah strikes back at Rachel's success by giving Jacob yet another servant, Zilpah. Envy and strife produce envy and strife. It's a race to the bottom.[8]

If we're lazy readers, we might skim this passage and think, "Well, that was unseemly," and then move on. But Moses has just compressed lots of time. These few verses span years, perhaps even a decade or two. So the terrible rivalry between Leah and Rachel defines Jacob's life. It shapes the world into which the twelve tribes of Israel are born. Asher, Gad, Naphtali, Dan, Judah, Levi, Simeon, Reuben. Eight sons by three women. It's worth remembering that before these were abstract tribal names they were human beings—many with different moms but all stuck in the same mess. And it's a mess that only intensifies once the whole process restarts on account of some mandrakes, a popular ancient Near Eastern fertility drug.

No one comes across well throughout this next episode (30:14–24). Rachel is spurred on by desperation, so she turns not to the Lord but to superstition. Leah treats her husband like a pawn in her grinding game of chess against her sister. Jacob allows himself to be treated as such. It's all bad all the way down. It's gross, yet God is gracious.

The Lord gives a few more sons to Leah, who comes out of childbearing retirement with Issachar and Zebulun (30:16–20). The meaning behind those names reveals she has forgotten what she once knew before she gave her life over to strife and one-upmanship. If this development bothers you or strikes you as false, then I would simply respond, "People are complicated and forgetful." We can believe two things at once even if we have to hold them in tension: Leah's realization

---

8. Thank you to my friend Jeremy Meeks for his reflections on this passage.

at the end of Genesis 29 is sincere, and her grasp on it weakens as the years go by. The Lord also gives her a daughter, Dinah. All of this is useful backstory for what's to come.

Again, it's gross, yet God is gracious, even to Rachel, the provocateur of all this wickedness. She finally gives birth to a son, Joseph, not because of Leah's mandrakes but because of the Lord's mercy. Moses couldn't be clearer about this: "Then God remembered Rachel; he listened to her and enabled her to conceive" (30:22). This miraculous son will become the final main character of Genesis—but not yet. For now, there are no lessons learned, no aha moments, no tearful turns to the Lord.

When we get to the end of this passage, we're left to wonder, "Can anything good possibly come out of this ripped-up family?" Well, believe it or not, this messy origin story has started to answer that question. Three of these kids will become particularly crucial: Joseph, Judah, and Dinah. These children of women at odds with one another will be woven into Israel's story of redemption, a story that ultimately offers hope to the world.[9]

But we're not there yet. For the story to move on, Jacob has to move on, too.

GENESIS 30:25-43 //
SUPERSTITION OR SOVEREIGNTY?

We've already observed how Jacob and Laban are both grifters, constantly looking to pull the wool over someone's eyes and take advantage of them. In this passage, both men act true to form, and so we end up with a good, old-fashioned ancient Near Eastern double cross. The details may bewilder us—what's going on with the speckles and the spots and the trees?—but the gist of the story is familiar.

---

9. I mean, I'm not about to spoil the whole thing, but here's one reference if you want a taste: Rev. 5:1–6.

Let's first make sure we understand the basic plot: Jacob wants to go home to his family (30:25–26), Laban doesn't want Jacob to leave because he's gotten rich from Jacob's work. So Laban basically says, "Name your price to stay" (30:27–28).[10] Jacob says, "Are you kidding me? Surely I've given you enough" (30:29–30). Laban seems to relent and Jacob asks for nothing except the speckled and spotted sheep, the speckled and spotted goats, and the black lambs. Why? Well, Jacob says he chose these because they're easy to spot (30:33). "Agreed," Laban says.

And then the double cross begins.

It starts with Laban's herd heist (30:35–36). He steals Jacob's portion of the flock and gives them to his own sons. It's surprising that Moses doesn't record Jacob's response to this wicked ploy. We'd expect him to be quite angry since he now faces an impossible predicament. Laban removed all the black lambs and mixed-color goats, so Jacob now cares for a flock presumably full of white animals. This raises a question: how on earth will he get any of what Laban promised him? I don't know much about sheep husbandry, but I do know that two pure-colored sheep aren't likely to produce a flock full of striped or streaked or spotted sheep.

Ever the entrepreneur, Jacob has an idea. And, to put it mildly, it's a bizarre one. He relies on a selective breeding process with a superstitious flair (30:37–43): peel some bark, put the striped sticks in the flock's trough, and that will result in a mating process that multiplies streaked or speckled or spotted young. This goofy, superstitious husbandry tactic repopulates Jacob's inheritance.

---

10. Laban says he "learned by divination" that the Lord has blessed him because of Jacob (30:27). What do we make of that? Is he lying? After all, when he met Abraham's servant way back in 24:31, the very first words out of his mouth are, "Come, you who are blessed by the LORD." So the second he laid his eyes on them, he knew this family had been blessed by the Lord without divination. So either he's lying by overspiritualizing the obvious effects of their arrangement in order to set Jacob up for one of his tricks, or Moses adds this detail so that we know Laban is so spiritually blind that he has to turn to sinful, stupid superstition in order to intuit what should have been obvious: the material blessings he noticed in Genesis 24 had in fact been mediated to him.

But how? Well, any farmer or shepherd could tell you it's not because of the almond tree bark. The Lord quite obviously has his hand in this. Jacob himself admits as much in the next passage (31:4–9). The result is a clever reversal of Laban's ploy: "So the weak animals went to Laban and the strong ones to Jacob" (30:42). It's this reversal of fortune that expedites Jacob's departure from Harran, which we'll read about next. For now, we can simply acknowledge that the Lord was tired of Laban's deceptive and blasphemous ploys, so he took away what Laban always held most dear: his stuff.

GENESIS 31 // FROM PADDAN ARAM TO CANAAN: A HOMECOMING

Following their tumble down the socioeconomic ladder, Laban and his sons now spend their days pouting and whining (31:1–2). This signals to Jacob that it's time to go home, for real this time. What also seems to be for real this time is Jacob's acknowledgment of what we've hopefully noticed as readers: the Lord has been protecting Jacob. No superstitious scheming undermines his sovereignty, no mandrake countermands his mercy. No good gift gets to Jacob or his father or his father's father apart from his grace. Jacob is right: "The God of my father has been with me"—just like he said he would be when Jacob left for Harran way back in Genesis 28 (28:15; cf. 33:5).

After at least a few decades under Laban's heavy thumb, Jacob hatches one last secret plot to take his wives and his children and all his possessions and head home to his father. This secret departure quickly turns into a standoff between Jacob and Laban.[11] Laban accuses Jacob of deception, of stealing from him not only his household gods but the privilege of a joyful send-off. Laban threatens

---

11. Moses doesn't tell us why Rachel stole these household idols. Perhaps she feared they would help Laban or perhaps she wanted to sell them once they got far enough away. She did seem, after all, to be worried about their household's finances (31:14–16).

him and says the only reason he won't hurt him is because the Lord appeared to him in a dream.

Jacob doesn't know that his wife is guilty of Laban's accusations. So while Laban is frantically searching for the household gods, we're left to wonder, "Will Rachel die because of her husband's rash vow?" Thankfully, no, because she uses her uncleanness as an excuse to keep the stolen gods hidden.

The whole affair of the stolen gods is meant to highlight, yet again, the unstoppable sovereignty of the Lord. Laban is on the hunt to find and save his gods, but he fails. They remain defenseless and unclean. The Lord, meanwhile, delivers his people at every turn.[12]

Moses concludes the Jacob-Laban section, which began way back in Genesis 29, with a series of speeches. Jacob is a boiling kettle. He can't stand another moment of mistreatment and deception (31:36–42). And yet he's finally found confidence in a satisfying conclusion: "If the God of my father, the God of Abraham and the Fear of Isaac, had not been with me, you would surely have sent me away empty-handed. But God has seen my hardship and the toil of my hands, and last night he rebuked you" (31:42).

Once blessed, Laban is now bereft. And he still doesn't get it: "All you see is mine" (31:43). No, it's not. The best he can do is strike an uneasy truce with Jacob before he heads home empty-handed—no daughters, no grandchildren, no household gods, nothing except whatever weakened flock Jacob left for him.

While he and Jacob are talking through their negotiated peace, Laban says, "May the God of Abraham and the God of Nahor, the God of *their* father, judge between us" (31:53, italics added). There's still an unbroken distance between him and the Lord, just as there's about to be an unbroken distance between him and the Lord's people. So he kisses his daughters and his grandkids and he returns home, never to be heard from again.

---

12. Thanks to Sam Emadi for this observation in episode 10 of *Bible Talk*.

What a shame. Laban could have taken a firm grasp on the blessings of Genesis 12 if only he had blessed Jacob and his God. "I will bless those who bless you, and whoever curses you I will curse." But instead, always enamored with the outward and the horizontal—always enamored with material blessings (24:30)—Laban lost it all. Like drinking water scooped up from a rushing river, he could satisfy himself for a while, but before long every last drop escaped from his hand.

Laban's life turns into a tragedy, which unfortunately paves the way for much of what's to come.

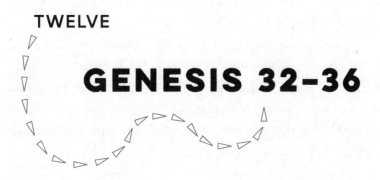

TWELVE

GENESIS 32-36

The lady doth protest too much, methinks.
—WILLIAM SHAKESPEARE, *HAMLET*

Gentlemen, you can't fight in here. This is the War Room!
—PRESIDENT MERKIN MUFFLEY, *DR. STRANGELOVE OR:*
HOW I LEARNED TO STOP WORRYING AND LOVE THE BOMB

Here's the last thing Moses told us about Jacob's relationship with his brother: "Esau held a grudge against Jacob because of the blessing his father had given him. He said to himself, 'The days of mourning for my father are near; then I will kill my brother Jacob'" (27:41). Moses has also told us that Esau is a "skillful hunter, a man of the open country" (25:27). Given all this, where would you expect Jacob to stop first on his homecoming tour?

GENESIS 32:1-23 //
A HORIZONTAL ATONEMENT

Wait, what! To Esau's house?

For better or worse, Jacob has always been a man of initiative, a "grab the feet by the heels" kind of guy. So it's not surprising that he's refusing to delay the inevitable. He's just accomplished a kind of detente with his decades-long enemy, Laban. So if he's going home, he might as well try to reconcile with his lifetime enemy, Esau.

Moses injects the first part of the story with some wry humor. He recalls Jacob's instructions to his messengers (32:3–5) but curiously skips over the messengers' interaction with Esau. Instead, he jumps right to their vague yet ominous summary: "We went to your brother Esau, and now he is coming to meet you, and four hundred men are with him" (32:6).

Gulp.

If you'd never read the Bible, you'd expect the next few paragraphs to retell a battle of brothers, like Cain and Abel, but with more armies and pent-up anger to resolve. That's what Jacob expects, too, so he starts divvying up his family and his flocks so they don't all die (32:7–8). You find out a lot about someone when they think they're surrounded by death—in funeral homes, in foxholes, in a figure-four leg lock.[1] When Jacob first heard the news of Esau's desire to kill him, he fled. What about now?

Well, he stays put and prays a beautiful prayer (32:9–12). Jacob is a different man.

Why is his prayer so beautiful? First, because Jacob acknowledges that the Lord's presence has been the reason for his prosperity (32:9).[2] Second, because he admits that everything he has is the result of God's kindness and faithfulness (32:10; Ex. 34:6). Third and finally, he bases his confidence not in his own cleverness and cunning but in God's covenant with Abraham and Isaac. (Compare 32:12 with 12:2 and 22:17.) Clearly, Jacob has come a long way from Genesis 28:18–22, when he made his confidence conditional.

---

1. Popularized by Ric Flair. This fits what's to come.

2. If you're not tracking, notice Jacob's interpretive twist of the Lord's specific command from 31:3. A bonus fact: this is also the first time Jacob refers to the Lord with his covenant name.

But just because Jacob trusts the Lord doesn't mean he fails to plan. His plan is a shrewd one: to intercept Esau's anger with a parade of presents. And when I say parade, don't picture your cul-de-sac's Fourth of July parade, marked by your neighbors halfheartedly waving some sparklers on the sidewalk. Picture something closer to the Macy's Thanksgiving Day Parade. Just look at the huge bounty he's offering: two hundred female goats and twenty male goats, two hundred ewes and twenty rams, thirty female camels with their young, forty cows and ten bulls, and twenty female donkeys and ten male donkeys (32:14–15).[3] These extravagant, expensive gifts are meant to accomplish an important goal. It would be imprecise to call this payback, as if Jacob can possibly—or if he even needs to—return the birthright he took all those years ago. Instead, it's better to think of these gifts as an offering to appease what he expects to be a very angry Esau. Moses' consistent use of sacrificial language in this passage means that we can reasonably summarize it like this: Jacob gives Esau a gift (an offering) to atone for his own past sins and to pacify (propitiate) Esau's present wrath. It's a horizontal, fraternal atonement.[4]

Again, if you'd never read Genesis before, the tension would be thick. Moses hides the resolution as long as he can: "So Jacob's gifts went on ahead of him, but he himself spent the night in the camp" (32:21). Then, under the cover of night, Jacob steals his family away across the Jabbok stream to what he hopes will be safety. He's afraid. He's alone. And then someone shows up ready to fight.

GENESIS 32:24-32 //
A VERTICAL FISTICUFFS

But it's not Esau!

---

3. Admittedly, this would be the strangest Macy's Thanksgiving Day Parade ever.

4. Thanks to both Jim and Sam, who noted this in our conversation. I think Gen. 30:20 is the clearest example of this principle. If you were fluent in Hebrew, you'd probably note with interest that Moses uses that word for "gift" nearly one hundred times in Leviticus.

Who is it? Why does Jacob want a blessing from him? What kind of witchcraft or wrestling prowess can pull off a finishing move like that?

The man is an angel who represents God himself.[5] He tells Jacob as much after their match is over (32:28). We saw something similar in Genesis 18 in the form of the three men before Abraham and Sarah. It's worth noting just how differently these two men respond: Abraham bows low to the ground and offers to serve these men dinner (18:1–5).[6] Jacob, well, that's not his speed. He doesn't bow down, he buckles up for a brawl. He's interested not in patronage but in pile drivers.

And so the two men wrestle through the night. For a moment or two, it seems like Jacob will prevail—until his angelic sparring partner pulls off a devastating finishing move: a flick to the hip. But even then, Jacob won't give up. The bell won't ring until the man gives Jacob a blessing.

Let's remember that Jacob doesn't know how this story ends. He's about to come face to face with his biggest fear, a fear that made him flee his home for twenty years. Let's also remember that his entire life has been marked by conflict—from the womb to the bedroom to the boardroom. From Esau to Rachel and Leah to Laban, Jacob's been fighting people his entire life.

And then, all of a sudden, he's alone and face to face with the Lord. The one he has to reckon with is not the ones he's been fighting. It's the Lord himself.

Why does he demand a blessing? After all, he just prayed a beautiful prayer that locates generations of promised blessings in himself. Why demand what he already has? Like his father and grandfather before

---

5. Some theologians have wanted to be more specific and say that these visits are not simply representatives of the Lord but appearances of a preincarnate Christ. While I'm sympathetic for the desire for specificity, such claims are overstated and ultimately blur the uniqueness of the incarnation.

6. In a similar situation in Josh. 5:13–15, Joshua takes his shoes off and falls facedown. Maybe in Genesis 32 the angel left his sword at home. Also, Hos. 12:3–4 comments on this passage, saying Jacob "struggled with God. He struggled with the angel and overcame him; he wept and begged for his favor."

him, Jacob is a complicated, mixed-up guy. Perhaps he's so afraid that he needs a final stroke of reassurance from whoever this is. Perhaps he's reasonably sure it's the Lord and so he's trying to squeeze him like a tube of toothpaste, making sure to get every last bit of blessing.[7] Whatever his motivation, by the end he's learned the right lesson: he's seen God face to face and lived. You can't leave an encounter like that unchanged. So he names the place after "the face of God," a fitting homage to that day's champion.

Moses ends the story at sunrise. It's a new day and Jacob has a new name: Israel.[8] Of course a passage that features a wrestling match also features a name change. No longer known as one who deceives others, he is now known as one who has struggled with the Lord. But there's another detail that deserves our attention, an indelible piece of proof that Jacob and the nation that bears his new name will never be the same. Here's how Moses closes the passage: "The sun rose above him as he passed Peniel, and he was limping because of his hip" (32:31).

Imagine you're one of Jacob's family members. You see him crossing the Jabbok at sunrise, anxious to face the day ahead. But before you hear about any encounter with any man, you see the proof. Before you hear about his new name, you see his new limp. I'm not simply drawing out this detail to get one of those evangelical *mmm*'s. You know what I'm talking about. We hear something in a sermon—something like, "The memorial of Jacob's weakness was to be with him as long as he lived, and how pleased would you and I be to go limping all our days as Jacob had, if we might also have the blessing that he won"[9]—and we remember everything the Lord's brought us through and we can't help but feel exactly like Jacob in this moment. Sure, we're limping, but we're limping to where the Lord's called us go to. *Mmm.*

---

7. Jacob realized this man represents the Lord without the man telling him, which makes me think he had a pretty good idea all along.

8. Moses uses the names Jacob and Israel more or less interchangeably throughout the rest of Genesis. Sometimes, he'll switch back and forth in the same passage (e.g., 37:1–3), so we shouldn't make too much of the different uses.

9. Okay, that's Spurgeon. I can't make up something that good!

But I'm not trying to pull a rhetorical fast one. I'm emphasizing what Moses emphasizes. Look at the passage again. He's got one more thing to tell us before he moves on to the long-awaited confrontation between Jacob and Esau: "Therefore to this day the Israelites do not eat the tendon attached to the socket of the hip, because the socket of Jacob's hip was touched near the tendon" (32:32). This is one of those verses our brains tend to blip past. But hang on! We should pay attention when Moses shifts perspective. It's as if he stops narrating Israel's past for a second to look his audience in the eye and explain a present-day custom that can't be found in the Torah. It's as if he's saying what Spurgeon said: "Jacob walked with a limp after his encounter with the Lord. In that same spirit, we refuse to eat the part of an animal that the Lord touched. It's hallowed ground."

GENESIS 33 // A SERIES OF Ps

Do you remember how Moses introduces Jacob and Esau? The Lord tells their mom:

> Two nations are in your womb,
>> and two peoples from within you will be separated;
> one people will be stronger than the other,
>> and the older will serve the younger.
>
> —*Genesis 25:23*

You could summarize their interactions with a series of Ps: there's the Prophecy, which we just mentioned. From the beginning we know Jacob and Esau are set up to be enemies. Then there's the Purchase (25:29–34), through which Jacob grifted his brother's birthright and through which Esau revealed his disinterest in the Lord. Step one of the separation is complete. Then there's the ominous Pairing (26:34–35): Esau marries two Hittite women, Judith and Basemath. These bitter marriages motivate Rebekah to devise Jacob's Pilfering[10] of Esau's blessing (27:1–41). This turns out to be the deathblow to an already strained relationship. Esau wants Jacob dead, so Jacob runs away for more than twenty years. That's where we've been—from the Lord's prophecy to Esau's purchase and pairing to Jacob's pilfering.

If you had to pick a word for what you'd expect next, what would it be? If Jacob's plan succeeds, then we could call it the Propitiation. Esau's wrath will be absorbed by the gifts from his brother. If it fails, then we might call Genesis 33 the Provocation. How could Esau be appeased by Jacob's traveling farm? He's out for vengeance.

But we get none of this. Moses plays with our expectations as long as he can, ratcheting up the tension with every detail: Esau's coming, and he's surrounded by four hundred men. Jacob bravely gets between the perceived threat and his family, even as he stupidly arranges them from most to least disposable.[11] He bows down before his brother as if Esau is the Lord himself and then—

Joy. Tears. Surprise. Even love?

Esau giddily meets his nephews and niece and seems shocked that Jacob would try to give him anything at all. Whatever anger he felt two decades ago has evaporated. The warmth of his response is shocking: "I already have plenty, my brother. Keep what you have for yourself" (33:9).

Jacob's persistent. He insists that Esau accept his offering.[12] Is this his guilty conscience speaking up? Perhaps. More likely, he doesn't fully trust Esau and wants to eliminate the possibility of being in his debt. Esau obliges and seems to suggest that Jacob's family can move in with his (33:12). That's how Jacob understands the request, since he

---

10. To keep up the series of Ps, I had to choose this somewhat stuck-up synonym for *steal*. I could have gone with Pirating, but it seemed a tad imprecise.

11. No detail is wasted. Jacob puts his favorite wife and son in the back of the caravan, where they'll be safest. Even here, at perhaps his boldest moment yet, Moses is sewing seeds for division within Jacob's family, which becomes the focus of the book's final act.

12. Again, Moses uses sacrificial language throughout this passage to underline Jacob's intention. When we read that Esau "accepted" the offering (33:11), passages like Lev. 1:4 and many, many others should reverberate in our minds.

tells him—after a mouthful of excuses—that he and his crew will get to Seir, eventually (33:14).

If you've ever said yes to someone you wanted to say no to, then you probably immediately saw through Jacob's accumulation of unnecessary information: "I'm sorry, our kids are so tired. Can you believe we forgot to let the dog out? I'm pretty sure we left the garage open." I know a flimsy, wordy excuse when I hear one. To spin the Bard's well-worn phrase, the man doth accept too much, methinks.

But Jacob's deception isn't just discoverable via rhetorical analysis. It's right there in the text, too. He tells Esau they'll eventually head to Seir. But we know he's on the road to the land of his fathers, his native land (31:3, 13). Jacob himself confirmed his commitment to the Lord's command the day before (32:9). Is he wavering? Or does he not trust Esau?

Thankfully, it's the latter. He stalls and stiff-arms his brother long enough to get out of sight and on to Sukkoth, where he settles down for a bit before planting his roots more permanently in Shechem (33:17–18). Shechem is where the Lord first promised Abraham that he would give him land (12:6–7). So Jacob is retracing his grandfather's footsteps.

Jacob signals his desire to settle down by buying a plot of land from the sons of Hamor (33:19). This should remind us of Abraham's wheeling and dealing with Ephron the Hittite to buy the cave of Machpelah for his dead wife (Genesis 23). Of course, Abraham bought the cave so that Sarah could die and be buried in it. Jacob buys this plot of land so that he and his many family members can live and multiply on it.

By the end of Genesis 33, Jacob is back home, and for the first time in his life, it's peaceful. He's dealt with Laban and Esau. We never hear from Laban again, and Esau makes only one more appearance. We were pretty hard on Jacob after he made a vow to the Lord that essentially amounted to, "I'll keep my end of the bargain if you keep yours" (28:20–21). What were his demands? Food to eat, clothes to wear, and peace to enjoy. Check, check, and check. The Lord proved himself to Jacob in ways he did not deserve. So Jacob keeps his word.

He plants roots in Shechem and, also for the first time in his life, builds an altar to celebrate the Lord's mighty works.[13]

When we started Genesis 33, we hoped for a propitiation and hoped to avoid a provocation. But in the end, we got something entirely unexpected: a Party between "reconciled" brothers and then a Praise service to the Lord. So take your pick for the title of this section: "The Party" or "The Praise Service."

Unfortunately, the party doesn't last long. The next story Moses tells is mired in sin and sorrow.

GENESIS 34 // UNSPEAKABLE OUTRAGE

Some passages of Scripture are tough to read because they're difficult to understand. Some passages are tough to read because they're so unfamiliar to our everyday experience. But some passages are tough to read because though they're both easy to understand and familiar, the events they depict are so terrible, so wicked, so worthy of our condemnation that we wonder why God saw fit to include them at all.

Genesis 34 is one of those passages. I don't think I need to rehash the sordid events in detail: Shechem raped Dinah and then sought to claim her as his wife. That's the inciting incident, another example of someone seeing and taking something that isn't theirs, which leads to disastrous consequences.[14]

Of course Shechem is the most vile offender in this passage, but he's not the only guilty party. Moses depicts Jacob as passive and ineffectual (34:5). He doesn't explain why Jacob responds this way, but it's worth noting that Dinah is Leah's daughter, not Rachel's. Perhaps he doesn't care for her as he should and therefore doesn't protect her as he should; he'd rather let her brothers get their hands dirty. Moses

---

13. What took Abraham a few verses—to build an altar at Shechem (12:7)—takes Jacob more than two decades. But still, we rejoice that he's a changed man.

14. For parallel passages, see Gen. 3:6; 13:10, 11; 16:3–4.

condemns Jacob's passivity subtly, but consistently. Though Jacob recedes to the background entirely after 34:6, he refers to "Jacob's sons" or "Jacob's daughter" six times from Genesis 34:7–27. He's there, but not there.

While Jacob chats with his daughter's rapist's father, Hamor, about the pros and cons of combining their families, his sons come home and burn with anger at the news.[15] Jacob should have been fighting for his daughter's reputation; instead, he's hearing a pitch from her wicked suitors.

I wonder what you thought as you read Hamor and Shechem's pitch (34:8–12). Of course it's a bad idea to wed yourself to a rapist and his family! But if we pay attention, we realize that Hamor and Shechem are trying to get Jacob's family to do something much worse than merely intermingle with a shady character. Look again. All the elements of the Lord's promise to Abraham, Isaac, and Jacob are there—land (34:10), seed enduring in peace and prosperity (34:9, 23), and blessing (translated "favor," 34:11). But they're on the lips of an enemy. There's a hiss in this proposal. It threatens to unravel the Lord's promises to Israel. "I will give you whatever you ask. . . . Only give me the young woman as my wife" (34:11–12). We should hear this offer and think to ourselves, *Nooo, don't do it!*[16]

Thankfully—but deceitfully—Jacob's sons speak up. Likely spurred on more by vengeance than adherence to the Lord's promises, they concoct a wicked plan. The Shechemites are susceptible because they're greedy (34:23). Again, I don't need to rehash the ruse in detail, but here's the gaudy headline: Simeon and Levi use circumcision, their sign of commitment to the Lord, as a tenderizer for terror. As my friend Sam summarized it, "This is like using baptism to drown people."[17]

---

15. Here's a fascinating connection: this same word for anger is used in 2 Sam. 12:5 when King David burns with anger in response to Nathan's parable. In both cases, there's a woman being mistreated. Of course, David's anger is hypocritical, while Jacob's sons' anger is justified.

16. We should hear an echo of the serpent in Genesis 3, and even of Satan's temptation of Jesus in Matt. 4:1–11.

17. *Bible Talk*, episode 12.

It's awful. It's a war crime. And it happens at the behest of Jacob's second- and third-born sons.

Though Jacob didn't have the Law,[18] Moses' original readers would have known it well. So it's useful to check out relevant passages like Deuteronomy 22:23–29, in which situations similar to Genesis 34 are addressed. Depending on the details, here's how Dinah's family should have responded:

- *Response 1 (following Deut. 22:25–27).* Shechem should have been killed because he raped a young woman "out in the country" who had "no one to rescue her." It's possible that's what's going on here, given how Moses opens this story in Genesis 34:1. Interestingly, this passage also manages to criticize those who "murder a neighbor," which is exactly what Levi and Simeon end up doing.
- *Response 2 (following Deut. 22:28–29).* Shechem should have paid the bride price and protected Dinah by marrying her as long as he lives.

Sure, Moses doesn't out-and-out say, "Levi and Simeon overreacted!" But if we embrace Moses' perspective and interpret this passage with what he writes later, then we know that whatever the right response should have been, it definitely shouldn't have looked like this. We can be sympathetic with these brothers' question—"Should he have treated our sister like a prostitute?"—and yet respond with one of our own: "Should you have treated the Shechemites like this?"

Why include this story at all? For at least two reasons. First, it explains how two of Leah's sons disqualify themselves—more on that in the coming chapters. Indeed, "Shechem had done an outrageous thing in Israel by sleeping with Jacob's daughter" (34:7). So, too, had Israel's sons by murdering these Shechemites in cold blood.

---

18. That is, Exodus, Leviticus, Numbers, and Deuteronomy.

Second, Genesis 34 highlights yet again that the patriarchs are not perfect people. The Lord is gracious and committed to his purposes, despite their commitment to sin.

GENESIS 35–36 // FULL-CIRCLE FINALITY

By the time we get to Genesis 37:1, Jacob will live "in the land where his father had stayed, the land of Canaan." But we're not there yet. Moses has got some tidying up to do.

First things first: the Lord urges Jacob to go back to Bethel, where he came across that angelic elevator on his way to Harran, where he and Jacob had their first interaction (28:10–22). With Moses' casual mention of household gods (35:2), we find yet another hint of Jacob's dwindling influence over his family.[19] He failed to protect Dinah, and now he failed at stomping out idolatry. We can trip up on this and think, "What was the point of that wrestling match? I thought Jacob trusted in the Lord!" To which I would simply say, yet again, that people are complicated. They're mixed up. Sinners sin, strugglers struggle, and the Lord is merciful to us all.

But why is Jacob going back to a place he's already been to learn some stuff he already knew and receive a name he already received? Because this passage is all about full-circle finality. He buries his household gods and then worships at Bethel. Then he buries Deborah, his final tie to his beloved mother, Rebekah (35:8).[20] Then the Lord puts on that record he gave Jacob back in Genesis 28—*Abraham's Greatest Hits*—and starts playing it again. The high points of Genesis 12, 15, 17, and 28 are all reasserted here.

Everything from here is distilled as Moses transitions from Jacob to

---

19. Perhaps Laban rubbed off on Jacob more than we'd realized.

20. It's surprising that Rebekah, such a central figure for this section of Genesis, doesn't even get an obituary. Presumably, she died while Jacob lived with Laban. Nonetheless, Moses notes Deborah's death to signal the death of Rebekah's influence in Jacob's life.

Jacob's sons. Rachel dies while giving birth to Benjamin (35:19). Jacob buries her in Bethlehem[21] and then moves on. It's during this season that Reuben—Leah's firstborn son—sleeps with Bilhah, Rachel's servant and Jacob's concubine (35:22). So if you've been keeping track, Leah's first three sons have now all done something stupid and therefore disqualified themselves as leaders of the family. Simeon and Levi are war criminals; Reuben disdains his father so much that he thinks he can seize the role of patriarch by sleeping with Bilhah, who is likely the "woman of the house" in Rachel's absence.

How has a man of such initiative lost control of his family? Though Moses doesn't answer this explicitly, he's dropped a few hints along the way: it all comes down to preferential treatment. We'll see the full flower of that sin in the chapters to come, but Moses has sown seeds of it already. We saw how Jacob failed to honor Dinah when Shechem defiled her. But do you remember Genesis 33:1–2? While facing potential death at the hands of Esau, Jacob arranges his family according to his affections. Perhaps Leah's sons have had enough. They're sick of their father and want nothing to do with his leadership, much less his "love." These tensions will ratchet up and eventually be resolved. But not yet. Jacob still has to finish his journey home, and when he gets home, he has to bury his father (35:27–29).

A long time ago, I mentioned that Moses treats genealogies as like Marty McFly treats Doc Brown's DeLorean—as a time machine. They teleport us forward and usually introduce a new main character. We haven't seen a genealogy since Ishmael's in Genesis 25:12–18, which Moses recorded immediately after Abraham's death. Notice the similar situation here. The death of the patriarch yet again provokes Moses to recall the line of the nonfavored son. Once Isaac dies, Moses immediately gives us Esau's genealogy.

By my count, this genealogy includes seventy-three different names, an impressive number. It includes folks like Oholibamah and Zepho,

---

21. Yes, she died in Bethlehem. No, I don't think that has massive significance.

Mizzah and Uz. We know next to nothing about these people. Like Ishmael's family in 25:18, we know where they end up: some distance from his brother, Jacob (36:6). We also know this genealogy is full of chiefs and kings.

And yet, if we've been paying attention, we'll realize this is one of the saddest chapters in the Bible. It's Esau's last appearance, the post-credits of his life.[22] And how does Moses describe him? He's rich and more or less reconciled to his brother. He's settled down in a faraway place, east of Eden. He's the patriarch of princes and kings. It won't be long before these kings will clutch their riches so tightly that they'll threaten the Lord's people with the sword (Num. 20:14–22). It won't be long before these brothers at odds become nations at war, just as the Lord prophesied.[23]

In Genesis 34, we saw how Jacob's sons rightly avoided assimilation but wrongly chose vengeance instead. In Genesis 36, we get a front-row seat to what assimilation would have looked like: prosperity and authority in a land far from the Lord.

Let's stop and think for a second so that we can see how, at the end of his life, Esau becomes a warning to us all. It might be tempting to think his life ends better than it started. The brother who stole the blessings from him—Esau forgives him. His mind changes from murder to mercy, from vengeance to love. But though he returned to and reconciled with his brother, he never returned to and reconciled with his God. Though he ended up prosperous and peaceful, his lack of concern for the things of God meant that the end of his life was marked with sadness, not success.

Sometimes, we think the worst thing that can happen to someone is that they rebel and run from the Lord and make a bunch of messes that they have to clean up later in life. I understand that. Some of my

---

22. There's another P. After the Party, there's the Postcredits.

23. Check out 1 Sam. 14:47, which comments on the situation in Numbers 20. And then of course there's the one-chapter-book Obadiah, which provides the final historical update on the Jacob-Esau relationship.

friends are still digging out of holes they started digging when they were teenagers. But that's not the worst thing that can happen. After all, the Lord often uses suffering and even the consequences of our sinful choices to remind us of our need for him. That's basically the story of Jacob. The worst thing isn't rebellion against the Lord and chaos in this life. It's apathy for the Lord and peace and prosperity in the less important parts of this life.

That's basically the story of Esau. The saddest imaginable outcome of someone's life is that they experience peace and prosperity with everyone except the God who made them.

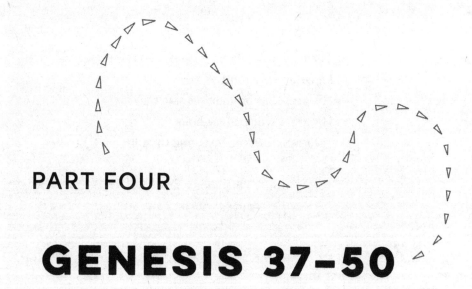

PART FOUR

GENESIS 37–50

Through many dangers, toils, and snares,
I have already come.
His grace has brought me safe thus far.
His grace will lead me home.

—JOHN NEWTON, "AMAZING GRACE"

I think I'll go home now.

—FORREST GUMP

THIRTEEN

GENESIS 37–41

> The interpretation of dreams is the royal road to a
> knowledge of the unconscious activities of the mind.
> —SIGMUND FREUD, *THE INTERPRETATION OF DREAMS*

> Life can only be understood backward,
> but it must be lived forward.
> —SØREN KIERKEGAARD

From now until the end of Genesis, Moses will finish his retelling of Israel's origin story. So far, we've tracked the lives of Abraham, Isaac, and Jacob. The Lord's promises and plan will succeed through these imperfect patriarchs. Who's the next link in the chain? Genesis 37–50 answers that question, and it includes many, many twists and turns.

To put it mildly, the situation with Jacob's sons is complicated. The first-, second-, and third-borns—all from Leah—have disqualified themselves. Reuben, Simeon, and Levi are out. The next oldest son from Leah is Judah. We'll meet him in a bit. Jacob's preferred wife, Rachel, is dead and buried in Bethlehem (35:18–19). She gave him only two sons: Joseph and Benjamin.

So which son will receive their great-grandfather's promises? Here are the leaders in the clubhouse: Judah, Joseph, and Benjamin. You will have to keep reading to find out this story's surprising resolution.

GENESIS 37 // SIBLING RIVALRY AND A SURPRISING RESURRECTION

Moses introduces Joseph's relationship to his family with a swirl of familiar tropes: there's sibling rivalry, there's superficial and preferential parenting, there's even a surprising prophetic dream. At the center of it all is Joseph. At first, he kind of seems like a try-hard tattletale, a bit of a pretentious punk. You can picture the scene: he's out in the field with his brothers. Something goes south, so he runs home—in his fancy coat, his "ornate robe" (37:3)[1]—to whine to his dad about his brothers. However Jacob receives Joseph's report, it's still more proof to the rest of his sons that "their father loved [Joseph] more than any of them" (37:4). So they hate him in silence (37:5).

Of course, Joseph doesn't deserve this. His father's stupid parenting strategy has made his beloved son the target of his siblings' scorn. And yet Joseph makes a bad situation worse when he—not once but twice—gathers his brothers around him and unambiguously prophesies that he, one of the youngest sons, will one day be his brothers' boss, and perhaps even their king.[2] This is so jaw-dropping that even Jacob manages to speak up and slow Joseph down (37:10). And yet, Moses tells us, Jacob "kept the matter in mind" (37:11). After all, once upon a time Jacob was the beneficiary of a surprising, role-reversing prophecy (25:23–26), and he has encountered the Lord in dreams before (28:12; 31:10–11).

---

1. The only other time this word gets used is in 2 Sam. 13:19. In that passage, King David's daughter Tamar tears the robe as a sign of her mourning and mistreatment by her brother. Perhaps this gives Joseph's coat a royal undertone, or perhaps it places him—like Tamar—in the place of a beloved child who is also being mistreated by his brothers. As we'll see, another robe he wears will get torn off, too, and used as "proof" of his destruction.

2. The details of the dream are straightforward: Joseph will be a king of creation as sun, moon, and stars bow down to him. This seems like a fulfillment of Gen. 17:6, when the Lord tells Abraham, "Kings will come from you."

Jacob's preferential treatment of Joseph goes beyond an ornate robe; he also gives his favorite son an outsized role. Based on Jacob's instructions in 37:12–14, it seems like Joseph works as a kind of go-between, a midlevel manager who's supposed to check on his brothers' work and report back to his dad. Perhaps, like Joseph's brothers, you also know what it's like to be managed by underqualified and overeager people. But to state the obvious, being overeager and underqualified doesn't mean you should get murdered. Joseph may lack discernment, but he doesn't deserve to die.

Nonetheless, his brothers lie in wait. While Jacob's dreaming about a coronation, they're calculating and calloused and ready to act in cold blood. Moses' small details speak volumes:

- This isn't a crime of passion but premeditation (37:18). A first-degree offense.
- They mock Joseph for his divine, self-designated dreams (37:19–20). Their dialogue feels almost ripped from a made-for-TV movie. I can see the villain snarling and twirling his mustache: "Then we'll see what will become of his *dreams*" (37:20).[3]
- Reuben comes up with a different plan (37:21–22). "Rather than killing him and getting blood all over our hands, let's just throw him down this well!" Moses tells us Reuben's motive: he wants to rescue Joseph and take him home (37:22). Perhaps he wants to get back into his father's good graces after sleeping with his concubine. But Reuben's half-baked plan fails, proving that he is still Jacob's ineffectual firstborn.
- Finally, Joseph's brothers strip him down and steal his robe, that perpetual sign of their father's sinful preference, the match that lit their perpetual fire of hatred. Then they hurl him into a waterless well (37:23–24).

---

3. I owe this comparison—of Joseph's brothers to a mustache-twirling villain—to Sam Emadi.

And that appears to be that. You can practically see them wiping the dust off their hands as they sit down for a nice dinner. Joseph is as good as dead.[4] He's turning to dust in a dried-up cistern. And then a better plan reveals itself. The brothers see a caravan of Ishmaelites up the road. I'll return to them in a moment. The fourthborn, Judah, one-ups the firstborn, Reuben: we can keep our hands clean *and* make a buck (37:26–27)! If Reuben is a feckless failure, then Judah is a sinister success. He is both self-serving and sinful.

By the time we get to the end of Genesis 37, Joseph has been sold into slavery for twenty pieces of silver.[5] The overlooked sons from the line of promise have given the favorite son to the Ishmaelites, the patriarch of the prodigals.[6] In an ironic twist of fate, Jacob's sons have tricked their father the same way Jacob once tricked his own father: through fabricated fabric (27:14ff.). Jacob is inconsolable. His son is dead, and he won't see him until he goes to the grave himself (37:35). The end seems fixed. Absent a resurrection, there is no hope.

A few reflections before we move on: First, sin is sticky. We've noted a few times how the sins of the parents are the sins of the progeny. Rebekah's sin sticks to Jacob; Jacob's sin sticks to his sons. Yes, Jacob has changed, but he's not perfect. Sin is sticky.

Second, sin isn't stationary. Hate can lead to human trafficking. The biggest sins start in the smallest of places. The most obvious sins start invisibly. The loudest sins start silently. One big sin leads to thousands of lesser sins to cover up the first one.

What's the result of all this? For the first time in Genesis, it's unclear which brother will receive the promise. They've nearly all disqualified themselves, and the only one who hasn't (except for maybe Benjamin) has been carted away to Egypt. He's in the belly of the beast.

---

4. In the Bible, and often in real life, pits lead to death. See Ps. 30:3.

5. Yes, Judas sold Jesus into the hands of the Sanhedrin for thirty pieces of silver. That's similar. But I'm not sure the similarity is significant.

6. Based on Moses' interchangeable use of the terms Ishmaelite and Midianite (37:25, 28), it seems that the wild branches from Abraham—beginning with Hagar and Keturah—have in some sense become one.

Moses is a masterful storyteller. Did you notice how many times the Lord is mentioned in Genesis 37? Zero. As Joseph goes from beloved son to suffering at the hands of his brothers to surviving in the house of Pharaoh's righthand man, it's as if the Lord has been absent the whole time. Through it all, we can practically see Moses smiling to himself as his tense narration raises the question, "How can the LORD possibly save his people from Egypt? How can he possibly still be in control?"

GENESIS 38 // FROM BAD TO WORSE

After Genesis 37, the only brother who looks impressive in the world's eyes is Judah. He's a man of initiative, someone who knows what he wants and goes after it.

Moses now shifts the story to tell us more about this man, and what we learn is reprehensible. The details are sordid, but straight-forward.[7] Like his great-uncle Ishmael and his uncle Esau, Judah has happily intermarried with the Canaanites. He seems to have been absorbed into their region and religion.[8] Judah has three sons: Er, Onan, and Shelah. Er married Tamar, and then, Moses tells us, the Lord puts Er to death simply because he is wicked (38:7). Clearly, this is a messed-up family.

What do you make of Judah's request to Onan? He wants him to sleep with his brother's wife. Is this wicked or wise, predatory or protective? Now, if we forget that Genesis is the first installment of a single book called the Torah, we might be confused. But Moses expects

---

7. I just searched this book for the other times I've used that adjective *sordid*. Two instances came up: first, Genesis 19 when Lot is raped by his daughters; and second, Genesis 34 when Dinah is raped by Shechem. Both are deserved. When we include Genesis 38, Judah is involved with two of Genesis' three sordid events.

8. We can be confident about the latter because of how much shrine prostitution seems to be a part of his family's normal, everyday life. In the ancient Near East, prostitution propped up the practice of other religions. Judah himself refers to Tamar as such in 38:21.

his readers to know the duty Judah refers to in 38:8, even if it's not spelled out in detail until Deuteronomy 25:5–10. You should probably flip to that passage so you're familiar with the principle. Come back once you've read it.

Do you see how Genesis 38 turns Deuteronomy 25's abstract principle into historical reality? Er dies without a son. Per Deuteronomy 25:5–6, that means Onan has the duty to give his sister-in-law a son. Though biologically Tamar's son will be Onan's, legally the son will be the late Er's. As a result, Er's widow, Tamar—who otherwise would have been vulnerable and alone—will enjoy both property and protection through her son. Though Deuteronomy hasn't been written down, Onan's duty is nonetheless clear—both for Moses' original audience and to Onan himself. While this practice, often referred to as "levirate marriage," protects widows, it also introduces a conflict of interest for those in Onan's shoes. By siring a son for his dead brother, he cuts into his own wife's and his own sons' future inheritance. He creates a drain on the family resources. It's this concern that fuels Onan's greedy decision. Because he "knew that the child would not be his," Moses tells us, he makes sure his participation in the process cannot result in pregnancy (38:9).

So the Lord kills him, too. Two wicked sons, two swift killings.

It didn't have to be this way. Deuteronomy 25:7–10 explains what happens when a man wants to pull an Onan and refuse his duty to his brother's widow. He gets spit on and embarrassed, but he does get to go on with his life, ashamed but alive. Far better to be a living member of the Family of the Unsandaled than to be dead.[9] But because Onan is happy with superficial obedience—because he wants the pleasure of the sex without the possibility of a son—the Lord puts him to death.

If only the story stopped there.

Judah promises Tamar another chance, this time with Shelah, the

---

9. That sentence will make no sense to you if you didn't do your homework and read Deut. 25:5–10.

thirdborn. But he doesn't mean it. He wonders whether Tamar will kill another one of his boys (38:11). And so he waits, long enough for it to become obvious to Tamar that her father-in-law, just like her brother-in-law, is guilty of superficial obedience (38:14). Judah is going through the motions but has no intention of following through.

Moses' narration of what happens next is unambiguous. Judah is a terrible man, so morally bankrupt that Tamar knows she will get his attention by dressing up like a prostitute. Their dalliance is laden with sadness: a no longer grieving widower (38:12) sleeps with a grieving widow in disguise (38:14, 19). Though they've both been marked by death, their union creates a double dose of life. Judah will father his grandsons.

Tamar knows Judah well enough to know that she will need some proof of her child's parentage (38:16–19).[10] She also knows he'll do whatever he can to protect himself because he refuses to protect others. His heartless hypocrisy is on full display when he hears about his daughter-in-law's prostitution and immediately calls for her death (38:24). Hypocrites are often legalists when it comes to other people's obedience.

Again, Judah is terrible. But what do we make of Tamar? After all, she dresses up like a prostitute to sleep with her father-in-law! She's just as wicked, right?

I'm not so sure. While I understand the gut-level assessment, before we evaluate Tamar's character, we need to read carefully. Remember, she was *owed* Onan's protection, or at least a public acknowledgement of his shameful refusal to do so. She was also owed Shelah's protection, but Judah reneged. So perhaps, after enduring slight after slight, Tamar sought protection from the next closest family member: her dead husband's father.[11] Moses wants the reader to know that Tamar

---

10. And yet again, appearance is used to deceive. She dresses up as a prostitute to trick him and then uses his staff and signet ring to convict him.

11. Admittedly, this is speculation. The Law doesn't address the scenario of what someone in Tamar's shoes can do when the men in her life are refusing to protect her.

didn't *become* a prostitute: "After she left, she took off her veil and put on her widow's clothes again" (38:19). Instead, she acted like one to get what she was owed.

I'm not sure I would argue that Tamar's decision represents a righteous act of faith, as if she did what she did to attach herself to the family of promise by any means necessary. And yet I'm struck by Moses' resolution, especially when I remember how the story goes from here. Pay special attention to Judah's response in the climax: "As she was being brought out, she sent a message to her father-in-law. 'I am pregnant by the man who owns these,' she said. And she added, 'See if you recognize whose seal and cord and staff these are.' Judah recognized them and said, 'She is more *righteous* than I, since I wouldn't give her to my son Shelah.' And he did not sleep with her again" (Gen. 38:25–26, emphasis added).

Judah is repentant. He immediately acknowledges his superficial obedience and begs his righteous daughter-in-law for forgiveness. This terrible situation reverberates throughout Judah's life. For now, I'll simply say he's now a changed man and leave it at that. But he'll show up again.

Tamar's story concludes with more twins: Perez and Zerah. It's yet another curious birth story in a book full of them. Zerah seems to be the firstborn and so he receives a scarlet thread around his wrist. But then, surprisingly, he pulls back and his brother, Perez, comes out first. So the son with the outward sign of favor turns out not to be the favored son. Hmm. Let's keep a pin in that little detail for now.

GENESIS 39:1–6A // FROM A NEW PARADISE TO ANOTHER PIT

In Genesis 38, Judah "left his brothers" (38:1) and buddied up with the unseemly Hirah of Adullam. Disaster ensued. He married a Canaanite, he watched his wicked sons die and leave his daughter-in-law bereft, and he singlehandedly destroyed his propped-up reputation.

Joseph, meanwhile, has been "taken down to Egypt" against his will. He's first sold by his brothers into the hands of his mortal enemies the Ishmaelites and then sold again into Potiphar's house, one of Pharaoh's righthand men, the mortal enemy of Moses' original audience. This contrast between Judah and Joseph is no accident: Judah is where he wants to be and around all the people he wants to be around, but his life is a complete mess. Joseph is not where he wants to be and around no one he wants to be around, and yet, Moses tells us, "the LORD was with Joseph so that he prospered, and he lived in the house of his Egyptian master. . . . His master saw that the LORD was with him and that the LORD gave him success in everything he did" (39:2–3).

Why does all this good stuff happen to Joseph? Because he knows how to win friends and influence people? No, Moses is unambiguous about the reason. He tells us five times: the Lord did it. The Lord was with him (39:2–3) and the Lord gave him success (39:3) and the Lord blessed Potiphar's house through Joseph (39:5). Remember what the Lord promised Abraham way back in Genesis 12? "All peoples on earth will be blessed through you" (12:3). Well, here in Genesis 39, a slice of that promise is being fulfilled for a slice of Egypt. Because Potiphar blesses Joseph, he receives the Lord's blessing.

If you've never read Genesis before, when you come across Genesis 39:1–6, you might think you're about to be flooded by a torrent of Joseph's triumphs. That's how Moses sets it up. You can practically see Joseph interpreting dreams and managing building projects and saving shaved cats from burning pyramids. He's a foreign slave who has rocketed up Egypt's social ladder—from Potiphar's slave to Potiphar's righthand man, from subservience to prominence.

Halfway through Genesis 39:6, the picture Moses paints of Joseph in Potiphar's house is something like the picture he painted of Adam in the garden of Eden.[12] Joseph is a ruler under the authority of a

---

12. No, the comparisons aren't exact. Potiphar stands analogous to the Lord not because he is like him in every respect but because he's the master of the house just as the Lord is the Master of the garden (and everything else, too).

glad master, he's got work to do and he's flourishing in it, and he has absolutely everything at his disposal. "Everything that is mine is yours," we imagine Potiphar telling Joseph. "Eat from any tree. Pick your favorite room. Find the comfort of any woman—any woman, of course, except for her."

GENESIS 39:6B-20B //
ANOTHER SERPENT IN THE GARDEN

Flip back to Genesis 3:1 for a second. Adam and Eve's honeymoon is interrupted by a serpent slithering into their all-inclusive paradise. Here's how Moses introduces the conflict: "Now the serpent was more crafty than any of the wild animals the LORD God had made" (3:1a). So he hisses, "Did God really say?"

Now flip back to Genesis 39. Here's how he introduces the conflict in Potiphar's house, that mini-Eden smuggled inside the rebel nation of Egypt: "Now Joseph was well-built and handsome, and after a while his master's wife took notice of Joseph and said, 'Come to bed with me!'" (39:6b–7). Hopefully you hear a hiss in her invitation. She didn't say it just once, but "day after day" (39:10) she tempted him with the only thing he couldn't have (39:9).

But unlike Adam and Eve, Joseph refuses.[13] I wonder if you caught his reasoning. Sure, he mentions his trusted status as one motivation (39:8–9). He's got a pretty good gig, and he doesn't want to get fired. But then he concludes, "How then"—given the status the Lord has granted him—"could I do such a thing and sin against my boss?" Wait. That's not what he says. He says, "How then could I do such a wicked thing and sin against God?"[14]

---

13. Unlike Adam in Genesis 3 and Abraham in Genesis 16, Joseph refuses to listen to the woman's voice.

14. This reminds me of David in Psalm 51. Though he failed to follow Joseph's example and took Uriah's wife, Bathsheba, he ultimately remembered Joseph's lesson amid his repentance: "Against you, you only, have I sinned and done what is evil in your sight" (Ps. 51:4). But,

Horizontal consequences are helpful motivators to temporary obedience. But they're insufficient for lasting faithfulness. Joseph kept the Lord at the forefront of his mind, so he was prepared to withstand temptation. Yes, he ultimately fled, but only after repeated resistance. So Genesis 39 doesn't teach us to fight temptation by fleeing our circumstances. Instead, it teaches us to fight temptation by keeping the Lord on the tips of our tongues. No, not as a *tsk-tsk-tsk* taskmaster who's eager to shame us when we sin but as the one who beckons us toward faithfulness, which may be hard and costly in the moment, but always, always, always leads to lasting blessings—eventually.[15]

We should underline that last word: <u>eventually</u>. Joseph's faithfulness is not immediately met with blessing. Once Potiphar's wife is spurned for the last time, she tries to destroy Joseph. Of course, her evidence for her sham accusation is a piece of clothing. She accuses the outsider wunderkind—twice she calls him "Hebrew," once she calls him "Hebrew slave"—of preying on her. And it's immediately clear that he has absolutely no recourse. In a matter of minutes, he's accused, accosted, and locked up. Moses doesn't even record his self-defense.

Let's track Joseph's arc so far: from the treasured son to the bottom of a well to the treasured servant to the bottom of a cell. Up down, up down, up down.

Faithfulness always leads to lasting blessing—eventually. That's what Joseph's story teaches us so far. But hang on. If we emphasize *eventually*, does that mean Joseph has lost access to any lasting blessing while he's rotting away in an Egyptian prison? Not at all. Moses reminds us of something Joseph never forgot: "But while Joseph was there in the prison, the LORD was with him; he showed him kindness and granted him favor in the eyes of the prison warden" (39:20b–21).

I must admit, there's something a bit sweeter about Joseph's response on instinct as opposed to David's poetic reconstruction.

15. I don't mean to deny the wisdom of fleeing particularly tempting circumstances. But we need to realize that this particular response is downstream from a heart that's settled in God's goodness.

What I'm about to write is so obvious, but it's worth stating explicitly. Joseph has never read Genesis. He has no clue how his story is going to turn out. All he can figure out at this point is that he's suffering for righteousness' sake.[16] He has every single reason in the world to complain and wither away, to shake his fist at the Lord and give up. But instead? He gets to work. At the end of Genesis 39, Moses describes a surprising replica of the Egyptian Eden. The prison receives the same blessings as Potiphar's house. Why? Because Joseph is there, and the Lord is with him (39:21, 23).[17]

GENESIS 40 // A DEAD-END DREAM

Moses stiff-arms our optimistic expectations once more. We end Genesis 39 and Joseph is on the up-and-up. Sure, he's ascending from the dungeon, but he's ascending nonetheless. And then Genesis 40 begins and the lights go out and the cloudless sky gives way to storms. It's "some time later" (40:1) and Joseph is still stuck in the clink. He's "confined," but with some measure of authority.[18] It still seems bad for him.

Countless threads had to be woven together to get here—all the stuff with Joseph that we've covered, the arrest of Pharaoh's baker and cupbearer,[19] and more—but by the end of Genesis 40:4, the table has been set for salvation, not only for Joseph but also for the entire nation

---

16. If you're preaching or teaching through Joseph's story, this would be a repeated on-ramp to connect Joseph to Jesus.

17. I simply wouldn't have understood these Joseph chapters without the wonderful wisdom of Sam Emadi, both through our conversations on them in *Bible Talk* (episodes 13–19) and from his published dissertation *From Prisoner to Prince*, which I just now realized has a similar title to this book! Great minds think alike.

18. He had these two prisoners "assigned" to him (40:4).

19. We don't really know what they did to get thrown in prison. While these jobs may seem menial to us, they would have been important for Pharaoh. He needs to trust the people who make his food and serve his wine. As the story goes on, it becomes clearer that one has been wrongly accused and one has likely been up to something.

of Israel. That will become increasingly clear from now until the end of the book.

I love the Lord's sense of humor. This mess began with Joseph's dreams that provoked his brothers' wrath (37:5–7). Now dreams show up again and Joseph is eager to give an interpretation. The cupbearer more or less dreams about getting his job back (40:9–11). What a good employee. Thankfully, Joseph has good news for him: "Within three days Pharaoh will lift up your head and restore you to your position" (40:13). Then Joseph has two requests: first, remember me, and, second, please get me out of here.[20]

The chief baker clearly likes what he hears, so he sidles up to Joseph and tells him about his own dream, which is decidedly less pleasant. He has more or less dreamed about birds scavenging his brains like bread. I'm not sure why the baker expects a positive interpretation for such a macabre scene, but he does. He surely recoils when Joseph tells him, in a verdict thick with irony, "In three days, Pharaoh will *also* lift up your head . . . from your body" (40:19).

Everything happens just as Joseph predicts (40:20–22). We aren't told why Pharaoh restores the cupbearer. Perhaps the ambiguous attempted poisoning—or whatever happened to get these two guys thrown in prison—had been solved. But those details don't matter. What matters is that the Lord has remained with Joseph, even in the bowels of a prison. And despite all odds, he's flourishing; despite all appearances to the contrary, he's precisely where he's supposed to be.

And then comes yet another departure from our optimistic expectations: "The chief cupbearer, however, did not remember Joseph; he forgot him" (40:23). I will repeat myself: Joseph doesn't know how his story ends. But Moses does. For Joseph, it's hard to imagine how this sad conclusion feels like anything other than a dead end. But Moses knows it's a detour.

---

20. That first request is particularly intriguing because it's the same language in Genesis 39:21. The Lord already treated him with "kindness," so he's asking this man to do the same.

GENESIS 41 // FROM THE
PIT TO THE PALACE

Two full years pass (41:1). That's 730 days. Then Moses tells us about another dream.[21] This time, Pharaoh is troubled by the psychedelic details: gaunt cows devour fat ones, scorched heads of grain swallow up healthy ones (41:2–7). It's all very *Alice in Wonderland*. Unfortunately, the chief cupbearer is a little slow on the uptake. It's not until Pharaoh exhausts all of Egypt's wisdom and power that he remembers the gifted, incarcerated Hebrew (41:9–13).[22]

By now in Joseph's story, we recognize this familiar setup. Joseph's going to save the day yet again. But notice how his confidence never veers toward himself because it's always on the Lord. There he stands before Pharaoh—shackles still on his wrists but with his freedom at his fingertips—and he utterly diminishes himself. Pharaoh asks Joseph for his résumé and he responds, "I cannot do it, but God will give Pharaoh the answer he desires" (41:16). When he's facing the temptation to sleep with another man's wife, the Lord is always at the forefront of his mind. When he's facing the temptation to hoard all the honor for himself, the Lord is always on his mind.

Again, Joseph predicts what will happen (41:25–32). In this case, the dreams are telling not two divergent stories but the same story through different images. There will be seven years of feasting followed by seven years of famine. If Pharaoh wants to avoid disaster, he must prepare now.

The scene is unbelievable. A few hours ago, Joseph was in "gen pop,"[23] a well-behaved member of the prison's hoi polloi. Now he's barking

---

21. With all this dream interpretation, you might be tempted to wonder, "Should I try to interpret my dreams like this?" No. You should have absolutely no confidence that you can come to the same level of clarity and certainty. Pursue faith, not Freud.

22. I enjoy the detail that Moses adds about Joseph defeating Egypt's magicians. After all, he will do the same a few hundred years later.

23. Short for "general population," commonly used to refer to prisoners who aren't in other areas like solitary confinement.

orders at the king. And yes, after showing off his discernment and wisdom, Joseph shrewdly recommends that Pharaoh find a "discerning and wise" man to help him (41:33). Joseph may be humble, but he's not stupid! He sees a way out, a way to do what he had hoped the cupbearer would do for him. But he's careful and not presumptuous. We should notice how much Joseph has grown since the beginning of Genesis 37, where he came across as a little punk. Years later, he's circumspect and shrewd. His hard circumstances haven't hardened him. Instead, they've matured him; they've prepared him for the work the Lord wants him do.

We're nearing the close of Joseph's opening act. It's been full of ups and downs, fits and starts. In just five chapters, he's been dead and buried *twice*—first in a barren well and then in a prison cell. He's been promoted and imprisoned and then promoted again. He's been forgotten. For dozens of months and hundreds of days and thousands of hours. His moments of blessing have been brief while his moments of sorrow have stuck. And yet through it all, he's been a model of faith. Of course, Moses never uses the words *faith* or *believe* or even *trust*. But he shows us time and time and time again that Joseph relies on the Lord above all else.

How does Genesis 41 wrap up? It's all positive. And this time, the torrent of triumphs doesn't dry up.

First, Joseph becomes the real prince of Egypt (41:41–44).[24] Pharaoh tells him, essentially, "You can have everything but the throne." It's hard not to snicker at this prohibition since, from Moses' historical vantage point, it's quite clear that even—or perhaps especially—Egypt's throne is under the Lord's thumb.

Second, Joseph gets a new name and a new family (41:45, 50–52). This one is a little tricky. Is Joseph acting like Ishmael and Esau and Judah here? Is this marriage a hint that he's leaving the Lord behind? A few reasons why we can answer no.

---

24. Said with the utmost respect to Brenda Chapman, Steve Hickner, and Simon Wells—the directors of DreamWorks' *The Prince of Egypt* (1998).

- First, there's nothing to come that would suggest that happens. Moses doesn't start telling us about the trials and tribulations of the Anubis-worshiping Zaphenath-Paneah.
- Second, Esau married a Canaanite because it displeased his father, whom he hated (28:6–9).[25] Judah "left his brothers" to find a wife. Ishmael's case is less straightforward, but Moses tells us that Hagar specifically went to Egypt to get him a wife (21:21). In every case, these men could have—and should have!—stayed home to marry. They chose not to. Joseph's situation is altogether different. He's obviously where the Lord has placed him. So his decision to marry the daughter of an Egyptian priest shouldn't be seen as suggestive or negative, despite how it sounds.
- Third, and finally, look at his kids' names. Manasseh means something like "forget" and Ephraim means something like "twice fruitful." Moses gives more context: Joseph seems to want to forget all the trouble that led to this moment, and perhaps even forget the members of his father's household who perpetrated it. At the same time, he also celebrated that he has been fruitful even in his land of suffering, his temporary home. These names are simultaneously an act of rebellion and an act of resolution. Rebellion against those sinners who've sought to harm him and rebellion against his "land of suffering," where he lives and where he will one day die. But it's also a nod toward resolution because he's moving toward what's ahead. He seems to have no enduring bitterness.

Moses tells us about Joseph's third triumph: he saves the world (41:46–49, 53–57). His wise and discerning plan enabled Egypt to become a blessing to the nations during a global famine. Moses

---

25. It's worth reminding us what we saw in chapter 9 in our discussion of Genesis 24: "This preference has nothing to do with ethnic bias and everything to do with religious belief; it has nothing to do with being ethnically intermingled but, to use a New Testament phrase, is about being 'unequally yoked.'"

reports, "And all the world came to Egypt to buy grain from Joseph, because the famine was severe everywhere" (41:57). Joseph's experiences in Potiphar's house and in an Egyptian prison were but a slice of Genesis 12 fulfillment; now that slice gets considerably bigger. Abraham's great-grandson has saved the world. Who knew *that* was the story Moses was telling? Moses is a masterful storyteller.

In Genesis 37–41, we see how the Lord meticulously employs his providence to bring about his merciful protection. He can redeem wicked acts—like being sold into slavery or being lied about or being forgotten—and use them as stepping-stones toward salvation. All of this happens to Joseph, and all of it paves the way for Joseph to save the world.

This all makes sense. But hang on. What's going on with Genesis 38? Why does Moses interrupt Joseph's narrative to include a messed-up story about Judah that seemingly adds nothing to the narrative?

Because Moses *has* read Genesis. I mean, of course he has—he wrote it. He knows how the story ends. He knows that Genesis isn't fundamentally about feeding the nations during a famine. It's about preserving the line of promise so that, one day, a seed of the woman will crush the head of the serpent. Even as he focuses on another complementary story for a while, he keeps his finger on the pulse of his primary plot.

Now, you might be thinking, surely the son of promise is Joseph, right? Right? He's Moses' main character. But more than that, he's a Hebrew almost-king (cf. 17:5) whose huge quantities of grain—"like the sand of the sea" (41:49; cf. 22:17)—have caused the nations to stream to Egypt so that they may be blessed by him.[26] The rest of his brothers are out of the picture. So surely all of this is just a preamble to Joseph's coronation as the next link in the chain.

Not so fast. What I think we have here through the rest of Genesis

---

26. Joseph is a royal figure and Moses depicts his accomplishments in terms that explicitly nod at Abrahamic fulfillment. See also Isa. 2:1–2ff.

is another Perez and Zerah situation (38:27–30), where the son who appeared first and received an outward sign of favor—well, it turns out he might not be the one. Because in the beautiful story of the Bible, the Lord not only redeems wicked acts, he also redeems wicked people. And those redeemed people actually change.[27]

As our guided tour of Genesis comes to a close, we get a front-row seat to how the Lord changed one wicked man and then placed a crown on his unworthy head and a scepter in his bloodless yet guilty hand. Indeed, Joseph has saved the world. He's started a family of his own. But now he needs to save his family so that one member of his family can eventually save him.

---

27. Thanks to Sam Emadi for this succinct summary of these chapters.

FOURTEEN

GENESIS 42-45

In New York, you can be a new man.

—ALEXANDER HAMILTON, *HAMILTON*

Well, well, well. How the turn tables.

—MICHAEL SCOTT, *THE OFFICE*

Since the sad end of Genesis 38, Moses has put the family drama on the back burner and instead focused on how Joseph's personal drama intersects with national, even global, drama. In these closing chapters of Genesis, we see how they all coincide.

GENESIS 42-44 // A TWO-PHASE TEST OF TEN BROTHERS

We haven't heard from Joseph's brothers (other than Judah) since they sold Joseph for a buck to their covenant-breaking cousins, the Ishmaelites. But now, since the famine has spread to Canaan, they're back on the scene, starving and hopeless. In need of help, Jacob sends ten of his remaining eleven sons to Egypt. Without them, he says, they're as good as dead (42:2).

Moses only briefly reintroduces these characters, but we quickly realize that not much has changed. Though close to twenty years have passed, Jacob still shows obvious partiality to his favorite son, Benjamin, and the rest of his sons are still too suspicious to warrant their father's trust (42:3–4). Joseph, meanwhile, couldn't be more different: he's gone from the bottom of a well to the "governor of the land." He's in charge of all grain production (42:6), which means their lives are now in the palm of his hand. The tables have turned. Only he can fill their empty bellies.

Why did this family break apart? Because Joseph's dreams were his brothers' worst nightmares. They mocked him when he predicted they would bow to him (37:7, 9). Given such a vehement refusal, it's ironic that they don't even notice when their worst nightmare becomes reality.[1] I love how Moses just gets right to it: before Joseph can even recognize them, they've bowed their faces to the dust (42:6–7).[2]

At this point, the narrative takes several unexpected turns. Joseph has been pretty predictable so far: he more or less always does the right thing. He tells the truth, and he interprets dreams. He is wise and discerning and effective wherever he goes. So everything that happens after "he recognized them" might take us by surprise. Why does he take a sudden "heel turn"?[3] Why does he falsely accuse his brothers of being spies and then, for the next few chapters, put them through an elaborate spectacle?

The key phrase in the passage comes in Genesis 42:15: "you will be tested."[4] Before he forgives his brothers, he needs to figure out whether they really are as honest as they say. Have they changed? Or are they

---

1. It's worth mentioning how their reunion by itself is proof of God's meticulous providence. Surely thousands of people came to Egypt every day. And yet Joseph was at the right place at the right time to see his brothers.
2. They do so four times in the narrative (42:6; 43:26, 28; 44:14).
3. This is wrestling jargon for "become a bad guy."
4. This should remind us of Genesis 22.

still the same wicked opportunists? The bulk of the next three chapters is devoted to the various phases of Joseph's test that will force them to answer that question once and for all.

PHASE 1: DO YOU WANT TO MAKE ANOTHER BLOODLESS BUCK? (42:15-43:15)

Joseph's plan unfolds in phases, but the goal is always the same: to test their character. Since they have another brother, Joseph tells them if they want to live, then they must bring him to Joseph safely. Remember, Benjamin is Joseph's beloved brother. Their kinship makes sense; they're the only sons of Rachel, the only wife Jacob loved. Before Joseph can forgive his ten half brothers, he must see his one full brother face to face.

Throughout this passage, Joseph carefully constructs a plan that reconstructs his tragic past. He tests his brothers by placing them in an identical situation to see if they will make an identical choice. I wonder if you caught it. Joseph tells them to leave one brother behind and return with Benjamin, whom they have left at home (42:19–20).[5] Joseph's brothers catch it; they immediately notice the eerie parallels: "Surely we are being punished because of our brother" (42:21). Which brother are they talking about? Joseph, the one who "pleaded with us for his life."

At this point, paranoia and finger-pointing take over. The brothers act like characters in a horror movie. When things go south and ghosts start spooking people or some mask-wearing maniac starts murdering people, that's when you hear hapless losers like Reuben yell, "Didn't I tell you not to . . . ? But you wouldn't listen!" (42:22). That's when people start trembling and asking, "What is this that God has done to us?" (42:28).[6]

---

5. Joseph started with a different plan: "Send one of your number to get your brother" (42:16). But that test would be too easy, so he switches the ratio. Is he making this up on the fly, or was it always the plan to change the plan? We don't know. A magician never shares his secrets.

6. They trembled, which is how Isaac responded when he heard about Jacob's stealing Esau's blessing (27:33).

But Joseph's reconstruction of their past tragedy isn't quite complete. He adds the perfect flourish: he gives them their silver back (42:25–28, 35). Now the reconstruction is complete and Joseph's brothers face a terrifying question: Do we want to make another bloodless buck?

These guys once chose to sell their brother for some silver and tell their dad that something else had happened. They supported their fabricated story with some bloody fabric. It worked once, so why not try it again? Sure, Simeon is wasting away in Egyptian confinement.[7] But Jacob doesn't know that. So they can make up another story. He got sick. He tripped and fell into a hole. He gotten eaten by a camel. Whatever. Thankfully, they see the Lord's heavy hand in all this. They can't explain *what's* happening to them, but they know exactly *why* it's happening: it's divine punishment for what they did to Joseph (42:28).

By the time they get home to Jacob, they realize the situation is worse than they've imagined. The silver's reappearance wasn't caused by a single administrative mix-up. No, this cursed currency has spread like cancer, and they are afraid (42:35). Jacob is despondent and thinking about death (42:38). He stubbornly refuses to do anything. The man of initiative has succumbed to inertia. His oldest son, Reuben, keeps saying stupid stuff. "Trust me to protect your kid," he says, "and if I fail, then you can kill my kids!" Real inspiring stuff (42:37).

At this point, a pall comes over the family of promise. I wish it were like a summer storm, intense yet brief. But these clouds stick, and no one does anything until they've run out of food. They let Simeon languish for weeks, if not months. Clearly Jacob would rather have Benjamin by his side even if it means another son rots. At first blush, it seems like they've failed phase 1 of Joseph's test not for greed or vengeance but for lack of trying.

And then Judah speaks up (43:3–5, 8–10). Yes, Judah! The first time we saw this guy, he was masterminding the plot to sell Joseph into

---

7. Why Simeon? Moses doesn't tell us. My guess is that Joseph is picking the brother who deserves it most. Simeon never faced repercussions for his slaughter of the Shechemites in Genesis 34.

slavery. The last time we saw him, he was signing his daughter-in-law's death warrant with one hand while holding proof of his own crime in his other.

But now? Two decades later, he's different. He's a changed man. He stares the situation square in the face and says, "We have to do something about this." Then notice what he offers as a pledge for Benjamin's safe return. Unlike Reuben, who offers his own kids, Judah offers himself (43:9).[8] Judah came on the scene as violent and self-serving. Now he's sacrificial.

What did we say at the end of the previous chapter? The Lord not only redeems wicked acts, he redeems wicked people. Perhaps Judah's assessment of Tamar—"She is more righteous than I" (38:26)—wasn't just a moment of guilt but the start of a new life.

Judah's speech convinces his father to let them take Benjamin on yet another trip to Egypt, where they will face yet another test. Jacob prepares a lavish gift for this greedy governor in Egypt, he begs God Almighty for mercy, and then he sends his sons—all ten of them—on their way (43:11–14).

PHASE 2: CAN WE STOMACH ANOTHER FAVORITE SON? (43:16-44:34)

Moses cuts straight to the brothers' second meeting with Joseph, and almost immediately the tension is resolved. They get off scot-free for the stolen silver. Joseph's brothers chat with his steward, and he tells them, "Your God, the God of your father, has given you treasure in your sacks" (43:23). The twinkle in his eye when he says that word *treasure* is practically blinding. Then Simeon gets released (43:23). Before we know it, they're sitting down for a meal with Joseph—they still have no clue he is their brother[9]—and he's giving them gifts. Oh, and they're bowing down again (43:26).

---

8. That word translated "I will guarantee" in 43:9 is the same root word that shows up in 38:18 as "pledge."

9. Maybe you're wondering, "How do they not recognize him!" Remember, in Genesis

From the brothers' perspective, the conversation is far from scintillating. Who loves answering a stranger's surface-level questions? But for Joseph, every update uncovers secrets from a long-lost past; every detail draws him back to a place he has assumed he will never see again. Seeing Benjamin pushes him over the edge. Moses tells us he is "deeply moved" (43:30), so much so that he cannot help but weep.[10]

Wait a second. I thought Joseph was pressuring his brothers with some sort of elaborate test. But this is the easiest test of all time! "Is your dad alive?" "Yes." "Is that the youngest brother you told me about?" "Also yes." "Great, you get an A plus. And I will let you live." "Thanks."

What's going on? Well, the test continues after the questions and with the command "serve the food" (43:31). Pay attention to how Moses describes the scene: Joseph eats by himself, the brothers eat by themselves, and then various Egyptian servants eat by themselves. There's no intermingling because Egyptians find it "detestable" to eat with Hebrews (43:32). Nonetheless, Joseph has reconstructed the seating chart so that they face him from oldest to youngest, from Reuben to Benjamin. That's not terribly surprising, but then Moses adds this "astonishing" detail: Benjamin has five times the amount of food! Yet again, the youngest brother receives the greatest blessing. The seating arrangement seems to "exacerbate their indignity."[11] But the party carries on (43:34).

Just like in phase 1, Joseph's not yet done. As they prepare to go home, he tells his steward to replenish his brothers' bags with food and silver. Then he tells his steward to add a silver cup to Benjamin's sack (44:1–2). We don't get the information we need to understand this

---

41:14 Joseph shaved himself and changed his clothes before interpreting Pharaoh's dreams. So it's safe to say he's dressing like an Egyptian and looks very different than he did as a middle-manager shepherd boy with a fancy coat.

10. In 43:14, Jacob prays that God Almighty would grant them mercy before Joseph so that Benjamin might survive. That's the same word translated as "deeply moved" in 43:30. So God answers his prayer. Mercy has come, and it's been mediated by Joseph. Thanks to Sam Emadi for this connection.

11. Jim Hamilton used these words to make this observation, and I couldn't agree more. Nor could I find a way to improve his characterization.

test until his steward runs them down the next morning and confronts them: "Why have you repaid good with evil? Isn't this the cup my master drinks from and also uses for divination? This is a wicked thing you have done" (44:4–5).

The point isn't that the cup is silver. He's already tested their greed and they've passed. The point is that the silver cup is used for divination, and it's about to be found in Benjamin's luggage.[12]

The elaborate process of uncovering evidence ends with Benjamin caught red handed. The brothers tear their clothes and head back to Egypt, certain that they're about to resign their father's favorite son to a fate eerily similar to Joseph's (44:11–13). Moses doesn't tell us whether they think Benjamin actually stole the cup. Based on their proposed suicide pact (44:9) and their confident participation in the steward's fact-finding mission (44:11), I'm inclined to think they trust one another. Even once Benjamin is "found out," they point to the Lord as the one who is primarily responsible for "uncovering [their] guilt" (44:16; cf. 42:28).

Joseph's brothers seem to be more worried about divine punishment than fraternal betrayal, so much so that Judah ups the ante and says they will all be his servants. Joseph refuses: "Far be it from me to do such a thing! Only the man who was found to have the cup will become my slave. The rest of you, go back to your father in peace" (44:17).

At this point, the second phase of the test is complete. More elements of their tragic past have been reconstructed in the present. And so they're met with another question: Can we stomach another favorite son? Joseph had the ornate robe; Benjamin has extra food. Joseph had divine dreams; Benjamin has the cup of divination. Will they abandon their brother yet again?

No, they won't, because Judah speaks up yet again (44:18–34). After rehashing the history of their conversations about Benjamin, he explains that if something happens to him, it would be catastrophic.

---

12. No, I don't think Joseph actually practices pagan divination. This is obviously a ruse, hence the reported premeditation.

He makes his case to Joseph entirely from the heart. Fourteen times he refers to his father. "It would kill him to lose Benjamin," he says. "So take me instead."

Judah so honors his father and loves his brother that he's willing to jeopardize his own future and safety and freedom for Benjamin's. He's willing to suffer and perhaps even die in his place.[13] Judah is an entirely new man, and Joseph can see it. Put simply, his brothers have passed the test.

Now it's Joseph's time to speak up.

GENESIS 45 // THE DAM BREAKS

"I am Joseph!" (45:3).

Why does Judah's speech cause Joseph to reveal himself? Because it proves a total reversal since Genesis 37. Joseph's past won't be repeated by Benjamin in the present. Joseph was the favorite son sold into slavery *by Judah*. Back in Genesis 37, Judah didn't care about his father, and certainly not his brother. So now, when Judah essentially says, "My life for Benjamin's; take me, not him," it's the clearest evidence of change that Joseph could have ever asked for. The book of Genesis has been full of brothers who either kill each other or want to kill each other. Finally, with this concluding set of siblings, we've moved from "fratricide to forgiveness."[14]

I'm convinced Joseph's exclamation is the climax of Genesis' final act (Genesis 37–50). Everything after this is resolution, which begins with Joseph's brothers. At first, they're terrified (45:3). But then Joseph comforts them not with mere sentiment but with theology he has learned in the "seminary of suffering."[15]

---

13. If you're preaching or teaching through Genesis, this would be an extremely straight-forward on-ramp to talk about how Jesus, from the line of Judah, has done the same for us.

14. I'm borrowing this phrase from Sam Emadi in episode 19 of *Bible Talk*.

15. I'm borrowing this phrase from Matt Emadi, brother of Sam. If the New England

But Joseph's seminary classes weren't like his ancestors'. After all, he's never directly interacted with Lord. He has never wrestled him to the ground or walked by him as a smoking pot and flaming torch. He has never heard his voice from the sky. The closest Joseph gets to direct contact with his divine teacher is when God helps him interpret a few dreams. Joseph may have been enrolled in this seminary of suffering, but he mostly took long-distance classes. He learned from stand-ins and substitutes; he never met the author of the assigned books.

Nevertheless, Joseph harbors no bitterness.[16] He's peered through providence and grasped by faith that, even through all the ups and downs, the Lord has never left him. In fact, according to Moses' retelling, Joseph followed the Lord more faithfully than all the previous patriarchs. His own father, at the end of his life, will remark that his years have been "few and difficult" (47:9). This sounds like a man filled with regret for his years of rebellion. Abraham and Isaac had similar episodes. They lied about their wives and slept with their servants and so on. And yet Moses records no such departures for Joseph. Was he perfect? Certainly not. But he remains a model of how to trust the Lord.

What do we do when our fears fog our vision so that we can't see the Lord? How do we respond when our suffering causes static so that we can't hear what we know to be true? We trust God anyway. Because he never, ever, ever leaves his people.

Joseph's comments in Genesis 45 prove that he's learned this difficult lesson. (See also 50:20.) He forgives his brothers because he knows the Lord used their sinful choices to put him in a place to save lives (45:5). He can see clearly that the Lord sent him to Egypt to "preserve . . . a

---

Patriots are the greatest football dynasty of all time, then the Emadis are the greatest Joseph-related, alliterated-pithiness dynasty of all time.

16. Of course, it's worth noting that Joseph wasn't naive as he pursued reconciliation. He moved slowly, carefully, which is absolutely okay. We must never be slow to forgive, even if we are slow to move toward restoration of a broken relationship. Forgiveness is a dish best served warm. Figuring all this out is hard, which is why we need godly friends and to be a part of a healthy church led by wise pastors.

remnant" (45:7). He knows that "it was not you who sent me here, but God" (45:8).[17] Though his brothers and the Ishmaelites and Potiphar's wife had their own devilish designs, though the cupbearer forgot him and his father mourned his death for decades, none of it could thwart the Lord's ultimate plan to save the world through Joseph.[18] A conflict that tore apart a family (Genesis 37) set in motion the solution for a conflict that threatened the whole world (Genesis 39–45). Through the Lord's meticulous and merciful dealings with Joseph, both have been resolved.

Throughout the rest of Genesis 45, Joseph sets up his family for future success. He gives them the land of Goshen (45:10), and then Moses tells us how the forgiven brothers respond to all this: "Afterward his brothers talked with him" (45:15). That might seem like a dud ending. Really? That's it? But it's not. It's yet more proof of reconciliation. Do you remember how Moses introduced their strife way back in Genesis 37? "They hated him and could not speak a kind word to him" (37:4). Sometimes a mere conversation is proof of a remarkable change of heart.

Then Joseph has one last mission for them: go home and get our father (45:16–25). This mission has no strings attached, no test at the end. When they get there and tell Jacob the good news—"Joseph is still alive!" (45:26)—he can't believe it. It's too good to be true. His beloved son was lost, but now he's found. He was dead, but now he's alive again. The news of Joseph's resurrection brings Jacob back to life (45:27).

And suddenly, the man of initiative is back, and he has only one thing left to do before he dies: "I have to go see my son" (45:28).

---

17. Joseph is more or less espousing the theological position called "compatibilism." Compatibilism teaches that God is entirely sovereign over all of human history. There's nothing that happens outside of his control or command. This doesn't mean he is the author of evil, nor does it mean that human beings do not make morally significant choices. See Acts 2:22–24 and Acts 4:27–28 for two similar New Testament passages. For more, see "Confession of a Reformed Philosopher: Why I Am a Compatibilist about Determinism and Moral Responsibility" by John C. Wingard.

18. In this, Joseph speaks better than he knows. He certainly is referring to how many lives he's saved during the famine. But it's also true that his actions preserved the line of promise, which make it possible for the Messiah to be born and save an altogether different group of people from an altogether different (but more serious) problem.

FIFTEEN

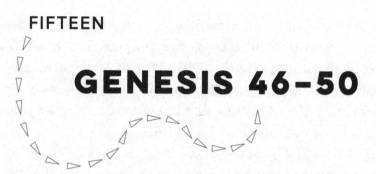

GENESIS 46-50

> I'll be back.
>
> –THE TERMINATOR

> Grace is glory begun, as glory is grace consummated.
>
> –FRANCIS TURRETIN, *INSTITUTES OF ELENCTIC THEOLOGY*

Our tour of Genesis is nearly over. As I said last chapter, the climax has already happened with the hearty reconciliation between Joseph and his brothers. Now we're waiting on a significant moment: the reunion of father and son. We've wanted to see this since the end of Genesis 37. More than twenty years have passed.

So, of course, it's the perfect time for Genesis' final genealogy.[1]

GENESIS 46:1-27 // ONE LAST GENEALOGY

Way back in Genesis 12, during another famine, Abraham went down to Egypt for help, and let's just say things didn't go well (12:10–20).

---

1. Moses is a masterful storyteller?

Abraham lied about who Sarah was, and Pharaoh's household got afflicted with disease. In Genesis 26, during yet another famine, the Lord appeared to Isaac and explicitly said, "Don't go to Egypt" (26:1–2).

So here we are again: another patriarch is in the throes of another famine and on the cusp of another journey to Egypt. This time, the Lord shows up to authorize the trip (46:3). He tells Jacob they'll stay long enough to become a great nation, even if it won't become their permanent home. The Lord tells Jacob, "You're going to die there, but one day I will bring your ancestors back" (46:3–4).

I've said before that genealogies are time machines, devices by which Moses fast-forwards to his next set of characters. But this one has a different function. It details all the people from whom these ancestors will come, the seeds who will be planted in Egypt to grow into a great nation (46:8–27).

Moses arranges the offspring list according to Jacob's wives. He begins with Leah's thirty-three sons and grandsons. Then Zilpah's sons and grandsons. She is Leah's servant, and Moses lists sixteen ancestors for her, less than half of Leah's. Then he transitions to Rachel's sons and grandsons; rather conspicuously, she's the only mother Moses lists before her children, which is likely his way of acknowledging her privileged status as the beloved wife. Her offspring number fourteen. Moses concludes his list with Bilhah's offspring. Similar to Zilpah's, she has seven ancestors, exactly half as many as her mistress, Rachel.

These people—seventy in all—are the seeds that will become the nation of Israel.[2] Though they will be planted in Egyptian soil, they will one day be uprooted and return home.

---

2. I'm not super into numerology—in finding significance in similar sets of numbers—but the connection between this list and Genesis 10's Table of Nations—which also features seventy names—is too curious not to mention.

GENESIS 46:28-47:12 // A PERFECT SETTLEMENT FOR DETESTABLE PEOPLE

Moses doesn't tell stories like we would. He devotes about 2,000 percent more real estate to an organized list of unfamiliar names than he does to the emotional reunion between Jacob and Joseph. And then Jacob wraps up the anticipated moment by saying, "Okay, I'm ready to die now." Moses then transitions to lots of chitchat about how Egyptians think shepherds—and therefore Joseph's brothers—are detestable.

We don't need to be overly concerned with the details. We don't need to know why Egyptians think this way, or why Joseph took only five of his brothers to Pharaoh. Joseph's goal in these interactions is to make sure Pharaoh lets his family settle in Goshen. It's the perfect place for detestable shepherds. Of course, because he's Joseph, his plan succeeds (47:6).

The passage ends with a brief, yet jaw-dropping scene. I originally titled this subsection "A Conversation between Two Kings" because surely a conversation between Pharaoh and one of Israel's patriarchs is significant. But it's secondary to Moses' main goal at the moment, which is to establish how the nascent nation of Israel gets settled in Egypt.

We've been with Jacob for half the book of Genesis. He's an old man who's been ready to die for a long, long time. So Pharaoh's opening question is understandable: "How old are you?" (47:8). He's 130. Then, as old men do, Jacob proceeds to tell Pharaoh a few things about his life. It's been hard; it's been a constant pilgrimage. But now, on the heels of finally settling down in a surprising place, the head of Israel proceeds to bless the head of Egypt before he leaves his presence and prepares to die (47:9-10).

In Genesis 47:1-12, Moses subtly portrays how the Lord uses the weak things to shame the strong. The detestable shepherds will grow into a great nation; Pharaoh himself grants them land in order to do so. Meanwhile, the king of the world's superpower sits across from a decrepit, depressed old man who has the audacity to bless him. We expect the strong leader to bless the weak man. But in God's economy, blessing runs from Jacob to Pharaoh. Any blessings Pharaoh enjoys at all—the breath in his lungs, the food in his belly—are because of Jacob's son Joseph. This Pharaoh ought to be commended for allowing Joseph and his family to flourish in his country. But he has no idea what he's gotten himself into by letting them settle down in Goshen.

GENESIS 47:13–31 //
MOSES ISN'T A MARXIST

When I first read this passage, I imagined how some might mangle it as an apology for communism. I can see it now: Pharaoh owns all the means of production (47:20), which leads to the saving of many lives (47:25). Of course, that's not at all what's going on here. Moses isn't a Marxist.[3]

Far from being an ode to the power of a particular ideology, this passage teaches us about the impotence of godless ideologies. It teaches us that salvation and survival cannot be found in political power structures or Egyptian infrastructure. It can be found only through the seed of Abraham and the protection he provides. Egypt doesn't save Israel here, Israel saves Egypt. "You have saved our lives," they say, not to Pharaoh but to Joseph.[4]

By Genesis 47:27, the Israelites are fully and finally settled in

---

3. Feels like we could sell merchandise with this mantra. The words are original to me, but I'm grateful for Jim, who explained the sentiment in episode 18 of *Bible Talk*.

4. This passage does raise the question of slavery in the Old Testament. We'll talk about that issue when we discuss Exodus 21 in the next volume of this series, which will cover Exodus through Deuteronomy (title TBD). Consider this footnote my version of an after-credits stinger: "Moses will return . . ."

Goshen.[5] Way back in Genesis 1:28, the Lord commanded Adam and Eve to be fruitful and multiply. He repeated that command to Noah (Adam 2.0) in Genesis 9:1. In Genesis 12:2 and 17:6, God told Abraham that he will make him fruitful. Here, for the first time in Genesis, God's people are simply described as "fruitful and increased greatly in number" (47:27). It's not a command. It's not a future promise. It's a present-day reality.[6] The Abrahamic promises are being fulfilled. Not completely, of course. They're in Egypt, not the promised land. But the sparks of fulfillment are flying up and will eventually set the whole nation of Egypt ablaze.

Genesis 47 concludes with a reminder that the Israelites' settlement isn't final. Shockingly, Jacob lives in Egypt seventeen more years. Before he dies, he makes Joseph swear to him that he will treat him with kindness and compassion by not burying him in Egypt (47:29).[7] Forget their golden, bejeweled sarcophaguses. Jacob doesn't want one. He wants to be buried not in foreign soil but in the little slice of land his family owns. He wants his plot in the Cave of Machpelah.

What's going on here? Does Jacob just have a sentimental attachment to his granddad's dirt? No, dust can't be sentimental about dirt. Jacob makes this request because he doesn't think he'll just become dust when he dies. He believes he'll live again. He trusts that even death can't destroy the Lord's promises. Death isn't the end of hope but the beginning of joy. We might say, in the words of the author of Hebrews, that "all these people [including Jacob] were still living by faith when they died. They did not receive the things promised; they only saw them and welcomed them from a distance, admitting that they were foreigners and strangers on earth" (Heb. 11:13). Jacob so trusted the

---

5. Did you notice what Moses calls Joseph's brothers? "The Israelites." Their status as a future nature is in view throughout these verses.

6. Thank you, yet again, to Sam Emadi for these observations.

7. When Jacob asks Joseph to put his hand under his thigh (47:29), we're reminded of Gen. 24:2, where Abraham asked his servant to do the same thing before he went to find Isaac a wife. Just as Abraham wanted his son to be married in the family of promise, so Jacob wants to be buried in the land of promise.

Lord that he wanted his burial to reveal that he saw and welcomed, even from a distance, all that had been promised to him.[8]

But before he's covered in dirt, he has a few blessings left to dispense.

GENESIS 48 // GRANDSONS GRAFTED INTO THE FAMILY

Using the genealogy in Genesis 46:8–25, I wonder if you could name the twelve tribes of Israel. They're all there. But unless you know this story and already know which two sons of Jacob are subtracted from the list, I suspect you'd get only ten out of twelve right.[9] Genesis 48 tells the story of how Jacob's grandsons and Joseph's sons Manasseh and Ephraim get included among the twelve tribes. Strictly speaking, there is no tribe of Joseph; instead, Ephraim and Manasseh are two half tribes that stand in his place. It's no surprise that Jacob gives Joseph the largest tribal representation, even if not all of Joseph's sons will be treated this way (48:6).

By now, Jacob really is knocking at death's door. He can barely stand and barely see (47:31; 48:10). But he still wants to bless his young grandsons. That's what the ceremony in Genesis 48 is all about. In Joseph's mind, the righthand blessing is supposed to go to the firstborn, Manasseh, while the lefthand blessing is supposed to go to the younger, Ephraim. Once Joseph realizes that Jacob is about to do the opposite, he thinks his blind-as-a-bat father has made an honest mistake. So he grabs his hands to correct him.

This is the first time that Joseph has made an obvious blunder.

---

8. Hebrews 11 is a bit of a skeleton key to help us understand the internal logic of Old Testament figures, especially the patriarchs.

9. Here's the list: Reuben, Simeon, Levi, Judah, Issachar, Zebulun, Gad, Asher, Joseph, Benjamin, Dan, Naphtali, Ephraim, and Manasseh. Twelve sons plus two grandsons equals fourteen. Joseph gets pulled out in favor of his two sons, making thirteen, and Levi inherits no land but rather becomes the priestly line of Israel.

He has succumbed to ignorance. Though he corrects his father gently, he does so on the basis of presumptuous, even worldly logic. For a moment, he forgets his own history, and certainly the histories of his father and his grandfather. Put simply, the Lord blesses the unexpected. He's not bound by cultural norms or expectations. So if he wants to place Ephraim before Manasseh—or Jacob before Esau, or Isaac before Ishmael, or King David before King Saul—then he can.

It's worth mentioning that when Moses refers to "blessings" in Genesis, he's not referring to well-wishes or best guesses. Jacob is a prophet, so these blessings are prophetic oracles from the Lord. Jacob doesn't know everything—for example, for twenty years he had no clue that Joseph was alive—but in certain key moments he's able to peer into the future with the Lord's help and make pronouncements about what's to come. Surely Joseph, ever the student of the Lord's providence, should know better. Far from being an expression of his father's senility, this surprising moment is an expression of the Lord's sovereignty. He's the one who will "bless these boys," the one who will ensure that they follow the footsteps of Abraham and Isaac as they "increase greatly on the earth" (48:16). Clearly, Jacob's grandsons aren't meant to be given a new set of promises but are to be grafted onto the same ones that Moses has tracked since the beginning of Genesis.[10]

GENESIS 49 // A LIST OF APPROPRIATE BLESSINGS

In Genesis 46, Moses arranges the sons of Jacob according to their mothers as they process into Egypt—it goes Leah, Zilpah, Rachel,

---

10. I don't know where else to put this information, but I have no idea what Jacob is talking about when he mentions the ridge he took from the Amorites with his sword and bow (48:22). Though we've been with him for half the book of Genesis, there's so much we don't know about his life!

Bilhah. The list in Genesis 49 is also arranged according to these mothers, but in a different order:

> *Sons of Leah (49:3–15)*
> > *Son of Bilhah, Rachel's Servant (49:16–17)*
> > > *Sons of Zilpah, Leah's Servant (49:18–20)*
> > *Son of Bilhah, Rachel's Servant (49:21)*
> *Sons of Rachel (49:22–27)*

Of course he saves his favorite sons from his beloved wife for last.

We often refer to what Jacob does here as blessing, but when we pay attention to the details we realize that in some cases, these blessings sound more like curses. Or, as Moses' says, they are "appropriate" blessings (49:28). Reuben, for example, is reminded of his lowest moment (49:4; cf. 35:22). Simeon and Levi are, too (49:5–7; cf. Genesis 34).

We'll return to Judah in a moment. After brief predictions for Zebulun, Issachar, Dan, Gad, Asher, and Naphtali (49:13–21), Jacob pauses for Joseph. These are his final words to his beloved son. He poetically characterizes his life as one who experienced extreme trial—from archers who shot at him with hatred in their eyes—and yet remained fruitful and steady because he knew the Lord was with him (49:22–26). He is the prince among his brothers, who will be blessed forever and ever, above and below, from the mountains to the hills.

Perhaps in Joseph, Jacob sees what he wishes he'd been all along. He once said "few and evil" had been his days (47:9 ESV). Jacob knows that he's made his own life hard. His sins have come home to roost. His deception wrecked his relationship with his brother; his favoritism wrecked his relationship with his sons; the wife he loved died and was buried in an unmarked grave beside the road (48:7). He's swallowed so much sadness that he wishes he'd died a long, long time ago. And yet here he is at the end of his life blessing his favorite, faithful son, and he can't help but stack up superlatives for the way the Lord has cared for him as his Shepherd, his Rock, his Mighty One, the Almighty whose hand always blesses and helps his people.

The blessing party abruptly ends with an ominous prediction about Benjamin (49:27). I wonder whether it hurt Jacob to be so honest.[11]

Now let's return to what Jacob says about Judah. It's the high point of the passage (49:8–12). At first, when we read his comments about brothers praising and sons bowing, his prophecy sounds like what we've already heard about Joseph (49:8). But there are other details for Judah that seem novel:

- His hand will be over his enemies' necks (49:8), which reminds us of a heel crushing a head (3:15).
- The scepter and the ruler's staff—signs of royalty—will not depart from Judah, at least until "he to whom it belongs shall come." When that happens, Jacob says, "the obedience of the nations shall be [Judah's]" (49:10). Obedience to Judah has expanded from his father's sons to all the peoples. Hmm.
- Finally, this descendant of Judah will tie his donkey to the choicest vine and wash his garments in wine (49:11). In other words, his reign will produce such abundance and prosperity that it doesn't matter whether the donkey eats the best grapes. During the reign of this descendant of Judah, we can treat wine like water and use it for something as lame as laundry.[12] His reign produces absolute abundance.

If this is the first time you've read through the book of Genesis, then I bet you thought this whole time—perhaps up until Genesis 49:10—that Joseph was the next link in the chain of promise. After

---

11. The closest we get to clarity on this prediction is verses such as 1 Chron. 8:40 and 12:2. Also, King Saul is perhaps the Old Testament's most famous Benjaminite, and he does hunt King David like a ravenous wolf.

12. Perhaps we can even treat gold like asphalt and use it to pave our streets.

all, he's the wise and discerning one, the royal figure who receives the bowed-down honor of his brothers. Joseph is indeed great. He received an appropriate blessing. But that line we've been tracking—from Adam to Seth to Noah to Abraham to Isaac to Jacob—doesn't extend through Joseph. It extends through Judah!

Here's how the New Testament begins the story of Jesus:

This is the genealogy of Jesus the Messiah the son of David, the son of Abraham:

Abraham was the father of Isaac,
    Isaac the father of Jacob,
    Jacob the father of Judah and his brothers,
    Judah the father of Perez and Zerah, whose mother
        was Tamar,
    Perez the father of Hezron . . .

—Matthew 1:1–3

Do you remember how Judah's sons Perez and Zerah were born (38:27–30)? It's an odd little story. Zerah pokes his hand out of the womb first and so the midwife puts a scarlet thread around his wrist—a sign of his status as the firstborn, the favored son—but then, to everyone's surprise, Zerah retreats and his twin brother, Perez, appears first. He's the true favored son, even if he lacks the scarlet thread around his wrist.

As it turns out, Judah and Joseph are a lot like Perez and Zerah. Joseph seemed like the favored son, the one who even had a piece of clothing to prove his status. But it turns out he's not who we thought he was. Despite his ornate robe and princely role, he isn't the favorite son. Against all odds, Judah is. How can that be? Well, it's because the Lord redeems wicked acts, and the Lord redeems wicked people. And sometimes he even grants those wicked people the status of being the great-great-great-great-and-so-on-grandfather of the Messiah, the one whom Christians sometimes call the Lion of the Tribe of Judah.[13]

And with that, Jacob's life fully and finally fades to black. Israel is dead in Egypt.

GENESIS 50:1-21 // A TEMPORARY EXODUS, A FOREVER RECONCILIATION

Genesis's conclusion gives us a glimpse into a poignant past and a glorious future. After Jacob dies, the whole nation of Egypt joins God's people as they mourn the death of their patriarch, and Pharaoh happily obliges Jacob's request to be buried at home (50:1–6).

What happens next seems impossible to believe. Jacob's funeral procession—which requires a trek of a few hundred miles—is attended by the Egyptian higher-ups. Moses simply reports, "It was a very large company" (50:9). In fact, the crowd of mourners is so Egyptian that when the local Canaanites happen upon the ceremony, they mistake them as Egyptians (50:11).

Jacob's sons do what he asked; they bury their father in the Cave of Machpelah, for which their great-grandfather Abraham paid full freight way back in Genesis 23. And then Joseph—and everyone else who came with him—goes back to Egypt (50:12–14).

---

13. At the end of chapter 13, I wrote, "Joseph has saved the world. He's started a family of his own. But now he needs to save his family so that one member of his family can eventually save him." Hopefully that now makes sense.

A bit more reflection on this whole episode: Have you ever noticed how the book of Ruth is essentially the happy inverse Genesis 38? Onan refuses to be Tamar's kinsmen redeemer, so she takes the situation into her own hands. The fallout is terrible even if God is able to redeem it. Boaz is the anti-Onan. He absorbs Ruth's problem. He provides for her, even though she's from Moab. The details aren't identical, but both stories end in the same, surprising place: the extension of the messianic line. In Tamar's case, we're talking about the no-name Perez. In Ruth's, of course, we're talking about King David (Ruth 4:22). Oh, one more thing: the author of Ruth seems to agree when he connects Ruth and Boaz directly to, you guessed it, Judah and Tamar. He even records that the elders and people of Bethlehem ask the Lord to make Ruth's house "like the house of Perez" (4:12 ESV).

We realize this is a poignant glimpse into the past when we put ourselves in the shoes of Moses' original audience. Perhaps they read this passage and wondered, "What if our relationship with Egypt had always been marked by such harmony?" Perhaps they read this passage and pleaded with Joseph not to go back to Egypt because they knew what would happen in the years between Joseph's peace and their enslavement. Whatever the case, this first, temporary exodus doesn't last.[14]

We might expect Moses' first installment of the Torah to end here, with the death and burial of Israel's final proper patriarch. But like *The Lord of the Rings: The Return of the King*, Genesis employs a few fake-out fade-outs.

Moses keeps writing. For a moment, Joseph's brothers wonder whether their brother's forgiveness was all a mirage to appease their dying dad. Somewhat hilariously, they forge a forgiveness demand, which breaks Joseph's heart (50:15–18).

Joseph reassures his brothers by offering them a summary of what he's learned throughout his life. I'm not sure whether thesis statements were popular in the ancient Near East, but if they were, this might be Moses': "Don't be afraid. Am I in the place of God? You intended to harm me, but God intended it for good to accomplish what is now being done, the saving of many lives" (50:19–20).

As we close our tour of Genesis, we should realize how the story of Joseph temporarily but sincerely overturns what has plagued humanity since the garden of Eden. Adam thought he deserved to be "like God, knowing good and evil" (3:5). And yet here's Joseph. He understands that he absolutely is not God. As my friend Sam said, "He rejects the status Adam sought to grasp."[15] By attempting to hurl himself into the company of the Lord, Adam ushered sin and death into the world. But Joseph, by humbling himself before the Lord, saves many lives.

---

14. If you want to see a passage that depicts an Egyptian exodus that does last, check out Isaiah 19. In this oracle concerning Egypt, the Lord predicts both the Egyptians' destruction and their redemption.

15. *Bible Talk*, episode 19.

Joseph's brothers don't die at his hands, they live. They have nothing to be afraid of. He will provide for them (50:21). They will feast in his house forever. And so he speaks kindly to his brothers, the ones who once upon a time "could not speak a kind word to him" (37:4).[16]

Despite their fears, the reconciliation endures.

GENESIS 50:22-26 // FROM EGYPT TO EDEN

Moses fast-forwards here without his usual genealogy. He tells us that Joseph lived 110 years, long enough to bounce his great-great-great-grandchildren on his knees (50:23).

Before Joseph dies, he tells his brothers what his father told him decades earlier: the Lord will come to their aid and take them out of this place. But then he makes a different request. He doesn't want to be buried in the land of promise. The Cave of Machpelah can wait until the time is right (50:24–25).

And with this sentence, Moses concludes his masterpiece: "So Joseph died at the age of a hundred and ten. After they embalmed him, he was placed in a coffin in Egypt" (50:26). For now, Joseph's bones are in a box in the belly of the beast. But one day, they'll come home, from Egypt to Eden.

---

16. Moses is returning to what he introduced in 45:15. Moses, what a masterful storyteller!

AN AFTERWORD THAT EXPLAINS BOTH WHERE WE'VE BEEN AND WHERE WE'RE HEADED

What's past is prologue.

–ANTONIO, *THE TEMPEST*

Apart from being casually referenced in this book, what do Jack Shephard from *Lost* and Forrest Gump from *Forrest Gump* have in common? They both want to go back. Jack wants to go back *in time* because it's the only way to fix his present-day problems. Forrest wants to go back *home* because, well, he's tired of running.

Genesis is neither as confusing as J. J. Abrams' TV show nor as sentimental as Robert Zemeckis's film. But it does carry within its bones a similar impulse: humans need a do-over, another chance. We need to go back, not in time, because that's impossible, but back home, to those fleeting moments in Genesis 1–2 when God walked with us in the cool of the day, when husband and wife stood naked and without shame.

In Genesis 3, we get the first drumbeat of how the Lord plans to get us there: a seed of the woman, he tells us, will finally prevail over the seed of the serpent. By the time we get to Genesis 12, the Lord—after thwarting the name-obsessed worshipers at Babel—says he will make a name for Abram. Indeed, he will bless all the nations of the earth through this one man. At this point, the promise of Genesis 3 both expands in scope and narrows in application.

From Genesis 12 until Genesis 50, we walk alongside the first four generations of this blessed family tree. We track the promises of God, wondering when and how they will be fulfilled. This story takes a number of shocking turns, but every detour eventually gathers itself toward the main destination: the Lord's keeping his promise to Adam, to Abram, to Isaac and Jacob and Judah, and so on.

By the end of the book, the nascent nation of Israel is settled in Goshen. That's good. But the patriarch of Israel is dead and buried in Egypt. That's bad. So they have land, seed, and blessing—precisely what the Lord promised to them—but the land is leased to them by a man whose crown looks like a king cobra's.[1] So the seed isn't safe, and the blessing they've extended to Egypt through Joseph's ingenuity seems temporary and tenuous at best.

It's worth remembering that just as Genesis is ancient history for us, it's nearly ancient history for Moses' original audience. More than four hundred years pass between Genesis 50 and Exodus 1.[2] Consider that four hundred years ago the ink on William's Shakespeare's *The Tempest* had been dry for only one year.

And yet by the end of Genesis, all the pieces are in play for Moses to finish his story. The past is indeed prologue, certainly for God's people. By giving us a selective yet detailed narration of his nation's backstory, Moses has told us all we need to know for what's to come.

As patriarchs, Abraham and Isaac and Jacob and so on were stand-ins for the whole nation of Israel. These men were regularly forced to answer the question, "Lord, do I trust you?" In Exodus through

---

1. Google "Uraeus" for more information.
2. Some folks argue about this even though Genesis 15:13 and Acts 7:6 seem pretty clear. But even on the shorter end, the least amount of time between the events of Genesis 1 and the exodus from Egypt is about 330 years. How recent does the reign of William and Mary feel to you?

Deuteronomy—and, really, for the rest of the Old Testament—that's the question Israel faces. But after four hundred years of fruitful multiplication, they have become exactly what the Lord promised to Abraham hundreds of years before. They've become a great nation, and they're too numerous for a single stand-in to represent the whole.[3] They must deal with the Lord themselves.

Flip back to page 206 and footnote 4. I wasn't kidding. We really are going to keep this guided tour of the Torah going. Having made the trek from Eden to Egypt, we'll prepare to make another one: from the silence of God to the singing of his people.

I hope you'll join me. Because Moses is a masterful storyteller, and the story is only just now beginning.

---

3. *Wait,* you say, *what about Moses!* Nope, he's from Levi's line, not Judah's. So he serves as Israel's priestly mediator, not their representative in the same way Abraham and his line do. If that doesn't make sense to you, well, then I guess you'll have to read the sequel.

ACKNOWLEDGMENTS

"It's been my pleasure. Thank you."

—JOE PESCI ACCEPTING HIS ACADEMY AWARD

FOR BEST SUPPORTING ACTOR[1]

Oh, wow. I feel like I just won an Academy Award. There are so many people to thank. Where do I begin?

The first person is obvious: this book wouldn't exist without the patient prodding of my editor Ryan Pazdur. This book was your idea. Thanks for taking a chance on a no-name like me. I've already thanked Jim and Sam, but I should also thank both Jonathan Leeman and Ryan Townsend, my two bosses at 9Marks. They hired me when I was twenty-four-years-old and knew basically nothing about everything. You've cared for me as bosses and friends, and it's been one of the honors of my life to work alongside you.

Thanks to Brian Phipps for your keen editing, and for not leaving Track Changes on so I didn't whine when you killed my darlings. Thanks to Alexis De Weese, who stewarded the cover design process and is making sure that this book will actually find readers.

Thanks to Drew Allenspach, Nick Roark, Drew Bratcher, and John

---

1. This is his entire speech.

Sarver for reading early stages of this book's early chapters. Your comments improved the book at every turn. I'm sorry I stopped sending you updated drafts. I was under deadline. Thanks also to ChatGPT, which called an early draft of part 1 "engaging and accessible, presenting the stories and their theological implications in a contemporary and relatable manner." Your soulless yet accurate assessment put wind in my sails. Thanks to my friend Ben Terry for realizing that running it through ChatGPT would be funny.

Thanks to Steve Hussung, whose faithful, no-frills preaching first opened my eyes to the beauty and depth of God's Word. Thanks to John Schreiner for making sure I got up every Sunday to get to church.

Thanks to Caroline and Corey at Quills Coffee in Saint Matthews, whose smiles and check-ins and doubly caffeinated cortados spurred me on through many foggy and fruitless days.

Thanks to my dad, who made me think I could always do hard stuff and who constantly asked me, to the point of annoyance, "How's the book coming?" Thanks to my mom, who always wanted me to be a writer.

I feel like Halle Berry, and the orchestra pit is starting to play me off stage. Only a few more!

Thanks to Third Avenue Baptist Church, who allowed me to teach through the whole book of Genesis for more than a year as I wrote this book. Thanks to Third Avenue's youth group, who listened lovingly and patiently. Thanks to Greg Tarr, who listened critically. You all sharpened my thinking and my ability to communicate those thoughts clearly.

Thanks to Elliot, Johnny, and Zoë. You endured many long afternoons when Dad would have otherwise been home. I'm sorry about that. I wish I wrote faster. I'm not sure you even know this book exists, but I hope you will read it one day not because you want to know what your dad was up to all those months but because you want to know more about the God who made you. I love you all.

Finally, thanks to Mel. This book wouldn't exist without you because, without you, I'd be a totally different person in a totally different place. I love you most of all. This book both begins and ends with an ode to you, the most lovely and remarkable woman on the planet.

That means this book is a chiasm.

—ALEX DUKE, October 2024

APPENDIX 1

	Genesis 6–9	Genesis 19
Sexual relations with angels	6:1–4: Angels come to earth and have sexual relationships with women.	19:1–5: Angels come to Sodom and the men of Sodom want to have relations with them.
Finding favor	6:8: Noah finds favor in the eyes of the Lord.	19:19: Lot finds favor in the eyes of the Lord.
Righteousness	6:9; 7:1: Noah is a righteous man.	2 Peter 2:8: Lot is called a righteous man. Genesis 18:19: Abraham is to teach righteousness.
Destruction	6:13, 17; 9:11, 15: "And God said to Noah, 'I have determined to make an end of all flesh, for the earth is filled with violence through them. Behold, I will destroy them with the earth'" (6:13 ESV).	19:13–14, 29: "Get out of this place, because the LORD is about to destroy the city!" (19:14).
Preservation	6:19–20: "And of every living thing of all flesh, you shall bring two of every sort into the ark to keep them alive [תְיַ תְ הְ ל] with you. They shall be male and female" (ESV).	19:19: "Behold, your servant has found favor in your sight, and you have shown me great kindness in saving [תְיַ תְ הְ ל] my life. But I cannot escape to the hills, lest the disaster overtake me and I die" (ESV).

(continued)

	Genesis 6–9	Genesis 19
Entering in and closing the door	7:16: "And those that entered, male and female of all flesh, went in [אוב] as God had commanded him. And the LORD shut [סגר] him in" (ESV).	19:10: "But the men reached out their hands and brought [אוב] Lot into the house with them and shut [סגר] the door" (ESV).
Judgment by "rain"	7:4: "For in seven days I will send rain [טרמ] on the earth forty days and forty nights, and every living thing that I have made I will blot out from the face of the ground" (ESV).	19:24: "Then the LORD rained [מטר] on Sodom and Gomorrah sulfur and fire from the LORD out of heaven" (ESV).
God remembers	8:1: "God remembered Noah."	19:29: "God . . . remembered Abraham."
Mountain	8:4–5: "The ark came to rest on the mountains [ריםה] of Ararat."	19:17, 19, 30: "Escape to the hills [הָהָרה . . .]" (ESV).
Drunkenness	9:20–21: Noah plants a vineyard and gets drunk.	19:32, 34: Lot's daughters get Lot drunk off of wine.
Knowledge	9:24: Noah knows [ידע] what his son did.	19:33, 35: Lot does not know [ידע] what his daughters have done.
Sons who father nations hostile to Israel	9:25–27: A son is born, whom Noah curses and who becomes a hostile people to Israel.	19:37–38: Sons are born who become a hostile people to Israel.

Special thanks to Michael Emadi, who provided this chart from his lecture notes on Genesis. Referenced in *Bible Talk* podcast, episode 6: www.9marks.org/interview/on -sordid-sins-and-the-glimmer-of-grace-even-in- sodom-and-gomorrah-ep-6.

APPENDIX 2

Genesis 24: Preview of the Exodus		
Dwelling outside the land	Rebekah: the bride	Israel: the bride
Sending of a servant	Abraham's "servant" (probably Eliezer)	Moses, the "servant of the Lord"
Servant's reluctance to go	Genesis 24:5	Exodus 3:11
Reminder of God's covenant faithfulness to the servant	Genesis 24:7	Exodus 3:12–15
Servant proclaims the word of the master / the Lord	Genesis 24:34–49	Moses speaks the word of the Lord to Pharaoh
Angel of the Lord	Genesis 24:7, 40	Exodus 23:20, 23
Laban hesitates / Pharaoh hesitates	Genesis 24:55	Exodus 8:28–32
Securing a bride	Genesis 24:67	Israel, the bride of YHWH, in covenant with him

Exodus and Conquest Sequence in Genesis 26

1. Abrahamic promises (vv. 1–5)
2. Famine in the land (v. 1)
3. Sojourn / settling in a foreign land (v. 6ff.)
4. Accrual of wealth (vv. 12–14)
5. Multiplication and increased strength / "You have become too powerful for us" (v. 16; cf. Ex. 1:9 ESV, "Behold, the people of Israel are too many and too mighty for us.")
6. Conflict in the promised land with surrounding nations (vv. 17–21)
7. The Lord gives peace and "makes room" so that the seed can be "fruitful in the land" (v. 22 ESV; on "make room" [Hiphil, *rhb*], cf. Ex. 34:24; Deut. 12:20; 19:8)
8. Building an altar / calling on the name of the Lord
9. Blessed by the nations and a blessing to the nations

APPENDIX 3: A READING LIST FOR THE EAGER AND THE ERUDITE

God's Glory in Salvation through Judgment: A Biblical Theology (James M. Hamilton Jr.)

Genesis 1–11:26 (Kenneth Mathews)

Genesis 11:27–50:26 (Kenneth Mathews)

Stephen Dempster's Genesis study notes in *The Grace and Truth Study Bible*

Dominion and Dynasty: A Theology of the Hebrew Bible (Stephen G. Dempster)

Preaching Christ from Genesis (Sidney Greidanus)

Kingdom through Covenant: A Biblical-Theological Understanding of the Covenants (Peter J. Gentry and Stephen J. Wellum)

From Prisoner to Prince: The Joseph Story in Biblical Theology (Samuel Emadi)

SCRIPTURE INDEX

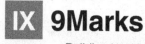 **9Marks**

Building Healthy Churches

IS YOUR CHURCH HEALTHY?

9Marks exists to equip church leaders with a biblical vision and practical resources for displaying God's glory to the nations through healthy churches.

To that end, we want to help churches grow in nine marks of health that are often overlooked:

1. Expositional Preaching
2. Gospel Doctrine
3. A Biblical Understanding of Conversion and Evangelism
4. Biblical Church Membership
5. Biblical Church Discipline
6. A Biblical Concern for Discipleship and Growth
7. Biblical Church Leadership
8. A Biblical Understanding of the Practice of Prayer
9. A Biblical Understanding and Practice of Missions

At 9Marks, we write articles, books, book reviews, and an online journal. We host conferences, record interviews and produce other resources to equip churches to display God's glory.

Visit our website to find content in **40+ languages** and sign up to receive our free online journal. See a complete list of our other language websites here:

9marks.org/international.

9marks.org